Not my idea
of heaven

D0928455

3027688

LINDSEY ROSA

Not my idea of heaven

The inspiring story of a young woman who
broke free from a strict religious sect
to find her own voice

harper
true

HarperTrue
HarperCollins *Publishers*
77–85 Fulham Palace Road,
Hammersmith, London W6 8JB

www.harpercollins.co.uk

First published by HarperTrue 2010

1 3 5 7 9 10 8 6 4 2

© Lindsey Rosa 2010

Lindsey Rosa asserts the moral right to
be identified as the author of this work

In order to protect privacy, some names
and locations have been changed.

A catalogue record of this book is
available from the British Library

ISBN 978-0-00-735434-4

Printed and bound in Great Britain by
Clays Ltd, St Ives plc

All rights reserved. No part of this publication may be
reproduced, stored in a retrieval system, or transmitted,
in any form or by any means, electronic, mechanical,
photocopying, recording or otherwise, without the prior
written permission of the publishers.

Mixed Sources
Product group from well-managed
forests and other controlled sources
www.fsc.org Cert no. SW-COC-001806
© 1996 Forest Stewardship Council

FSC is a non-profit international organisation established to promote the
responsible management of the world's forests. Products carrying the FSC
label are independently certified to assure consumers that they come
from forests that are managed to meet the social, economic and
ecological needs of present and future generations.

Find out more about HarperCollins and the environment at
www.harpercollins.co.uk/green

I dedicate this book to my gorgeous children,
Nina and Stanley; to Tom whose love has made my
life worth living; to my brother who has never wavered in
his support of me.

ABERDEENSHIRE LIBRARY & INFO SERV	
3027688	
Bertrams	17/11/2010
B ROS	£6.99

Contents

Contents

Preface

The world, as we understand it, exists in our minds. The problem is, we all think differently. To some people, the world I grew up in is perfectly normal. To them, it is right, and the way the rest of the people in the world live is wrong.

How you see it depends on which side of the fence you are standing.

I was born on the wrong side of the fence. This book is about my journey from one side to the other, and how I had to leave my family behind.

Although this is a true account of my life, I have changed the names of those involved to respect their privacy as much as possible.

Not my idea
of heaven

Chapter One

How Ever Did it Come to This?

My weight halved in a matter of months. The winter dragged by while I crouched against the radiator. I pressed my back into its heat until my skin burned. I sipped continuously from a mug of black coffee, willing the inky liquid to warm my bony body. Mum knelt in front of me, pleading, 'Please eat.' At last, desperate, she pushed crumbs of food into my mouth. I sealed my lips and turned my head away. Then the hunger came. I ate until I could eat no more. My belly, full of food, stretched and swelled, and I became consumed by rage. I used my fists to thump my face and jaw bone. So I sat on my hands while Mum fed me.

I became the prisoner of my mind. I listened carefully to its wild rants and became obedient to its command of weight loss. I purged my body of the pollutant, picking at my teeth to remove every last trace of food. But I wanted to be well, to be normal. How ever did it come to this?

Chapter Two

Welcome to My World

I sat in the Welfare office on the hard plastic chair behind the door. The windowless room was hot and I felt my sweaty legs sticking to the seat. The Asian boys messed around in the corner, scuffling with each other. I kept my head down and pretended to read my book. I didn't want anyone talking to me. It was embarrassing having to be there.

Through the open door I could hear the sound of my friends singing hymns in assembly. They were Christian hymns but I didn't recognize any of the tunes or the words. I just wanted to be with the other children, but neither their prayers nor their songs were approved by God. In my head I sang the words to a hymn that I knew would be.

Jesus bids us shine,
With a pure, clear light,
Like a little candle,
Burning in the night
In this world of darkness,
So let us shine –

You in your small corner,
And I in mine.

It comforted me. On rare occasions Mum would sit at the piano and ask me what songs I wanted her to play. I'd always pick 'Jesus Bids Us Shine' and 'Away in a Manger'. I stood by her elbow while she banged away at the keys and we sang together.

When the assembly was over, the Welfare lady sent us back to our classrooms to join in with the lessons. I could forget that I was different for a while, until the time for lunch came around. It was wrong to eat or drink with sinners. So I ate mine at home.

When I was old enough to read I was given a Bible. Not just any old bible: this one had my initials on the front, embossed in gold lettering. 'L.R.M.' The leather cover smelled expensive, not like the books Mum picked up from charity shops. This one was special.

I'd seen bibles at school, but I knew this one was different. On the first page was the name J. N. Darby. 'What does "Translated by …" mean?' I asked Mum.

She explained that Mr Darby was a very important man, because he had discovered the true meaning hidden in the Bible. 'The recovery of the truth,' she called it.

His picture stood on a shelf in our house, and had pride of place in every other home belonging to members of the Fellowship. People like us. There were other pictures too, which were also black-and-white shots of sober-looking men. These were the 'Elect Vessels', the men of God, chosen by Him to lead us.

We were the disciples. Those who had not discovered our truth were the 'worldly people'.

I knew it was wrong to mix with these people, who believed in devilish things and had Satan in their hearts, but they were all around us. We lived among them, but not with them. As my Bible said, 'Be in the world, but not of the world.'

We were special.

Special or not, I lived in a normal suburban street called Albion Avenue, lined by trees with rows of similar-looking semi-detached houses on either side. These were not Fellowship homes, they were full of worldly people, but my family somehow slotted in among them.

We were friendly enough to our neighbours. Mr and Mrs Harvey, the old couple next door, gave me and my sister Samantha chocolate treats and Mum chatted to them in the street, but our friendship ended on the doorstep.

The front garden of our house, number thirty-seven, was perhaps was a little more orderly than some of the others on the street. Mum loved gardening and took time creating neat rows of roses and irises. Other than a particularly tidy front garden there was not much to differentiate my house from any other. It all looked perfectly normal. But there was one small thing.

'My dad says your house hasn't got a TV aerial, so that means you haven't got a telly,' a boy living in my street blurted out one day.

'No,' I replied, 'we don't.' I felt proud, he looked shocked.

'Why not?'

I was blunt. 'Because it's my religion.'

'What do you do, if you don't watch telly?'

'Oh, we play games,' I said, and began the long list of exciting adventures that I got up to behind the door that was closed to all except the Fellowship.

'I play shops and offices and ...' I could see by his face that he was becoming envious of my tremendous life. I breathed a sigh of relief; he didn't think I was weird.

What I really did was play a lot on my own, creating an imaginary world from whatever was around me. I loved sneaking into the garage, pushing my way past the bikes and all the clutter, to find the door into the old coal cupboard where Mum kept her jam-making equipment. The shelves were stacked with jars, which I filled with potpourri and perfume, created using sticks to mash the flower petals I'd pinched from my mum's rose garden.

My dad's office was a wooden shed in the garden in which he designed aeroplane gearboxes for Rolls-Royce. His drawing board stood against the back wall, opposite the door. He'd roll out a huge sheet of drafting paper, tearing off lengths of masking tape to secure its corners, and begin to align his array of pencils on the parallel rule. I was fascinated with the meticulous detail in his drawings and loved watching them grow as I stood by his side, fiddling with the stationery in his desk drawer.

When Dad was out at work, I turned his office into a shop, opening the window to serve the customers. Tucked under a desk was a box of my sister's Cindy dolls, which I'd pull out and play with on the floor. As long as I didn't touch Dad's drawings, I was welcome to play in there any time I liked.

Being a design engineer, Dad could turn his hand to most practical tasks. A lot of the time he spent fixing the car, but he still managed to build a go-kart for me. If he was too busy, he was more than happy to provide us with some scraps of timber from the garage, and let us make our own entertainment. Armed with some of Dad's wood and a length of rope, my best friend Natalie and I made a crude swing, hung from a puny branch of a tree on our street. All we could do was swing one way and then the other. It was great, until the rope wore thin and snapped, and I landed on my bum.

Mum was always busy, too. She grew most of her own fruit and vegetables at the bottom of the back garden, freezing beans, and other crops, to feed us over winter. Every summer, the jam-making equipment would get dragged out of my favourite cupboard and Mum would set to work, preparing jar after jar of strawberry conserve, using the fruit we brought home from the pick-your-own farm.

How I loved spending a day there! I'd sit in the middle of the field saying, 'One for me, one for the basket, one for me, one for the basket.' On the way out I'd hide my face from the lady at the pay hut and try not to smile in case she saw the red stains on my cheeks and bits stuck between my teeth.

In many ways, my childhood was idyllic, but why wouldn't it be? My family and I had been chosen by God, so, of course, life was great. I knew that, whatever happened, the six of us would always be together, Mum, Dad, Alice, Victor, Samantha and me.

Chapter Three

One Size Fits All

The Fellowship didn't have churches with elaborate buttresses and elegant spires, just squat little meeting rooms with plain, windowless brick walls. The only way a worldly person could attend a meeting was by calling the number displayed on the board outside and making an appointment. It was very rare for anyone to do so, though. And, even if they did, they would be regarded with much suspicion. The high barbed-wire-topped fences and imposing padlocked gates were enough to put off most people.

Our meetings happened every weekday evening, once a month on Saturdays and three or four times throughout Sunday. We travelled far and wide to different meeting rooms, attending Gospel Preachings, Bible Readings, and gathering for prayer. Everyone in the Fellowship had to attend, but nobody minded. These were the great social events of our lives – the exciting part, really.

Nevertheless, they made dinnertime stressful. Dad had to make sure he was home from work on time and would usually come hurrying in, complaining about the terrible traffic on the M25. It didn't matter that Mum had four kids to look after, her job was to ensure the dinner was on the table in good time. Stuffing down the last mouthful of his pudding, Dad would jump up and, with a flurry of goodbyes, he was gone.

I usually went to meetings only on Sundays. The first one of the day was called the Supper, held in a small meeting room just around the corner from our house. I found it strange that something that started at six a.m. could be called that. As far as I understood it, supper was the name given to the meal that people ate in the evening.

We had to wake before dawn to make sure we had enough time to prepare. It took Mum absolutely ages to get ready. Sitting on a stool in front of the big dressing-table mirror, she'd watch herself pull back strands of long brown hair, and fasten it with a clasp. She used clips to tidy up the sides, then blasted the whole lot with hairspray to keep it in place. My sister Samantha and I would watch her, fascinated, waiting for our hair to be brushed and adorned in the same way.

Once at the meeting, thirty or forty of us sat on chairs arranged in a large semicircle, and began what was known as 'breaking bread'. The ritual involved a jug of wine and a wicker basket of bread, both of which were ceremoniously passed from person to person along the row. I always looked forward to my turn, so that I could gulp down mouthfuls of the beautifully sweet liquid, and feast myself on the doughy bread.

The lady who did the baking, Mrs Turner, had no idea that very few people actually liked her produce – no one in our Fellowship group had the heart to tell her straight. There was a detectable sense of relief in the room when she was ill and unable to bake. Personally, I loved the bread, although that was mainly because I was so hungry. None of us ate breakfast until after the meeting had finished, so, in order to satisfy our grumbling bellies, as soon as the meeting disbanded, and the parents shuffled outside into the little gravel car park to chat, the other children and I would wander through to the little kitchen and catch Mrs Turner before she tossed away her leftovers. It wouldn't have mattered what her bread tasted like: it felt like a treat to us. With our little hands full of crusts, we would head back out through the hall, stuffing the squashed balls of dough into our mouths.

I was awakened one Sunday morning with a terrible pain ravaging my mouth. The whole of my upper lip was swollen and I was in agony. Mum had to seek permission from the Fellowship before she was allowed stay at home and look after me. It turned out I had an abscess on my tooth, but I still felt as though I had done something very wrong by missing the meeting.

'God will understand,' Mum reassured me. She knew more about these things than I did.

Getting to know what God understood or disapproved of was important. Somewhere in the Bible it said that a woman praying with her head uncovered puts her head to shame, and the Fellowship took this message seriously. The solution they came up with was simple. For a start, every female wore a ribbon fastened with a clip. This showed God that we were one of His, and worthy of His protection. There was still the problem of the Devil to deal with, though. As soon as we were outside our homes and meeting rooms, he could reach us. Our protection was a headscarf, and a lot of Fellowship girls were made to wear them at all times outside their homes.

I wore a headscarf to meetings, but I was spared the embarrassment of having to wear it to school or out in the street. My worldly friends may not have been allowed in the house, but I played with them in our road and didn't want them to see me with that on my head. I told Mum, 'I'll wear it when I get older.' I meant it, too. I thought that, when I reached the age of sixteen or seventeen, I would be a grown-up, and when I was grown up it wouldn't matter if I was laughed at. I suppose I thought that Fellowship adults were immune to the stares and cruel comments made by people in the big bad world. Whenever I left the house, however, I made sure I had my token in my hair. Oh, apart from that one time.

It was a summer morning and I woke up in a wonderful mood. It was just after dawn and the house was still. There were no meetings to attend and not even Mum had stirred from her slumbers. The sun was already shining and I couldn't wait to go and play in the front garden. I dressed impatiently and brushed my hair straight in preparation for the elasticized hair band I was about to put on. Maybe it was because no one was awake to see me, I don't know, but for some reason, on that morning, I decided to find out what it felt like to go outside with nothing in my hair.

Standing in the hallway, door open, I stared at our silent street for a moment. Then, taking in a little gasp of air, I stepped outside, beyond the safety of the house. I didn't know what I expected to happen to me, but nothing did. So I went further, strolling down the concrete driveway, glancing left and right. I secretly wished that someone I knew would see me with my hair down, but it was too early and nobody was around. At the gate I stopped. I'd got only a few yards, but, when the realization of what I had just done hit me, I lost my nerve, dashed back into the house, closed the door, and quickly tied back my hair before anyone awoke.

Although I didn't like wearing my headscarf in the street, I was proud to do so at the meetings, where I fitted in with all the other girls. Mum had a whole box of square headscarves decorated with various patterns, and I hoped that one day I would have a full box just like that too. Instead, for the time being, I had to make do with my little plain lilac and pink versions. I often watched Mum carefully picking through hers, holding them up against herself to see if they matched what she was wearing.

Our clothing may have been restricted in style, but we went to town on making it as decorative as was possible within the boundaries we were set. I saw that my mum and sisters cared deeply about their appearance and knew that little details mattered a great deal to them.

Mum and Alice, who was fifteen years my senior, were always making dresses and skirts, and had become highly skilled in the art from their many years' experience. They had little choice but to make their own, because the clothes in the shops were either too fashionable or were meant for old ladies. We certainly didn't want to dress like old ladies, if we could help it, and fashionable usually meant too revealing. Skirts had to be respectably long – not necessarily all the way to the ankle, but definitely below the knee. A woman's knees and shoulders could never be shown. As far as trousers were concerned, they were for men only.

I especially loved trips to the haberdashery shop, where I ran around inspecting every roll of material. The main purpose of our visits was to find some material to make into a skirt, and, if I was lucky, it would be one for me. The material I really liked would typically be colourfully decorated with sprigs of flowers and suchlike, but I usually chickened out of my first choice and went for the one that I thought would make me less conspicuous when I played in my street. Something plain. It was hard to carry off a floral dress when my worldly friends were in their jeans and T-shirts.

Sometimes Mum would ask the shop assistant to cut her a metre length of quilt stuffing, and I soon got to know what she wanted it for. Mum had developed her very own, advanced technique for getting her headscarf to sit perfectly in place. To do this, she would start by cutting the thin layer of stuffing material into the shape of a triangle. Then, laying her scarf on the bed, she'd fold it diagonally and place the stuffing on top.

It was very important that she get it positioned just right so that it wouldn't show in the final arrangement. When satisfied with her preparations, in one flowing movement Mum would sweep the arrangement up and over in the air and flatten it down on her head, monitoring herself in the mirror as she did it. Sometimes she performed this manoeuvre five or six times before she got it just right. 'Right' meant no movement of the untrustworthy headscarf. I watched, impressed by her precision and attention to detail. The quilt stuffing inside stuck like glue to the layers of hairspray and packed out the scarf, making it look beautifully smooth. Next, a set of clips would go in. One last spray from the aerosol can and she was done.

No women in the Fellowship cut their hair. Mum sometimes trimmed my straggly ends and I felt – just for a few seconds – like a worldly girl. But there was no getting away from the fact I looked different. Every other girl I knew had bobbed hair or it was long but styled, whereas mine was very obviously a home job. It wasn't that it had been done badly, only that the fashions in the eighties were so extreme. Sometimes I sat in front of Mum's dressing table and held my long hair up so it looked as if it were short, or I pulled the ends over my head to make it look as though I had a fringe. Fringes were forbidden too, of course, as that involved cutting. It wasn't that I especially wanted short hair or a fringe. I just would have liked the choice to have been mine.

Men had an easier time with the Fellowship's dress code. They were forbidden from having long hair, moustaches or beards, but that hardly put them out of step with the fashions of the day. If anything, they just all looked middle-aged. On top they wore open-necked shirts, which were usually a sensible light blue or white. These were tucked into a pair of slacks cut in a classic style. It was all fairly standard stuff, but, when everything was added together, it pretty much amounted to a uniform. A worldly person would probably have trouble distinguishing a Fellowship man from a chartered accountant, but I could spot the difference a mile off!

Equality for women wasn't exactly a priority in the Fellowship. From the top down, everything was run by men, and, as far as the Fellowship was concerned, they were chosen by God. Nowhere was this more obvious than in the meeting rooms used for Bible readings.

We all sat on tiered rows of benches, which surrounded a central stage and a single microphone on a stand. Men were seated at the front, women and children behind. The men took turns speaking into the microphone, reading from the Bible, while the women tried to pay attention. This was difficult for us girls as we rummaged in handbags, hunting for pencils and paper to scribble notes on, chatting together in loud whispers.

Women weren't permitted to get up and speak during meetings. Their job was to announce the hymn numbers, and any woman was more than welcome to have a go at that. It meant standing up in front of everyone, and sometimes there was a long silence while the women looked at each other, hoping it didn't have to be them. The singing was started by the men, but, if the choir lead got it wrong, we'd all end up desperately screeching at the tops of our voices.

What I loved better than wine and bread was seeing Ester and her brother Gareth. He was my age, but 'Stelly', as I lovingly called her, was a couple of years older. I'd often go to their house to play, while my mum and some other Fellowship women gossiped in the kitchen. One time I was running madly around their house, playing a game of hide and seek. One by one I searched all the rooms, looking in every nook and cranny. I wasn't having any luck in the bedrooms, so I checked the loo. But when I peeked round the door and saw Gareth, I saw something else, too.

'Hi, Lindsey,' Gareth said.

I had never seen a boy with his trousers undone, and I revelled in my good fortune. The real ambition of a Fellowship girl was to get married and have loads of Fellowship children, and Gareth was the boy I'd already decided I'd marry when I was grown up. Now I could be certain.

That night when I said my prayers I thanked God for letting me see Gareth's willy. He certainly worked in mysterious ways.

Chapter Four

The Carpenter, the Dreamer, the Romantic and Me

When I was little, I shared a room with my sisters, Alice and Samantha. Our beds were lined up side by side, mine being the small one in the middle. There was just enough room to squeeze between them, but I didn't mind that it was cramped: I felt safe, flanked by my two big sisters. No bogeymen would come and get me in the night.

Our room had a very posh-looking set of fitted wardrobes covering one wall, but in the middle there was a recess to accommodate a little dressing table and its mirror. It was there that Alice sat to prepare herself for bed every night, but Samantha and I were rarely awake to see her. Being older, she attended the evening meetings, and Samantha and I had usually fallen asleep by the time she returned home.

One evening I awoke and saw her, lit by the little pull-string light above the dressing table, peering intently at herself in the mirror. I spied on her from beneath my blankets, hoping she wouldn't notice me. She was talking to herself gently, slowly plaiting her long hair. I watched her carefully secure two plaits with hair bands. Then came the part I remember most clearly. She opened the dressing table drawer and took out several curlers. These were not the old-fashioned tubes, but plastic clasps, covered in foam. Taking the tassel of hair that hung below her hair bands, she wrapped it around the curlers and fastened them. I shivered with excitement. How daring my big sister was! We were not supposed to try to make ourselves look pretty in any way. I wondered how she managed to sleep with those hard lumps on her pillow, but I guessed it must be worth it.

Alice really wanted to look her best because she was madly in love. She had met the man of her dreams – another Fellowship member. They had eyed each other during meetings, and, despite the seating plan, a Fellowship courtship had ensued. As far as anyone knew, Alice and Mike had never kissed or as much as held hands, but they did speak on the telephone. They spent hours talking each evening.

Young adults in the Fellowship typically met future spouses during a special three-day meeting that could take place in any country where Fellowship disciples were found. The Fellowship made no secret of the purpose of these events, which were a unique opportunity to widen the gene pool. Fellowship women were required to follow their husbands, which meant that as a woman you could end up living almost anywhere in the world. In Alice's case, she struck it lucky: her beau lived just around the corner!

Alice was so busy with her love affair that she failed to notice that everyone else her age was doing their GCE O-Levels and ended up leaving school with barely any qualifications. As it happens, this wasn't much of a problem.

Fellowship women were not expected to have careers, just a short stint working in a local office, as Alice did, and then on with the business of marriage. Their job was to reproduce and look after the household. The men were encouraged to gain skills as apprentices at Fellowship firms. University was out of the question, as it was seen as a place where subversive ideas circulated.

The biggest ambition we were expected to have was to get into Heaven. That was the dream.

If Alice was the romantic, Samantha was the dreamer. Actually, she was a romantic too. I can't say how she got on at school, being six years younger than she was, but academia was never her strong point. Still, if there was a qualification for fantasizing about romance and other lives, she'd probably score even better than I would.

I can only assume that Samantha's teachers gave her a hard time for doing badly in class, because that is what she gave me when we played teachers and pupils in one of our favourite games. Well, it didn't remain one of my favourites for very long, but she certainly liked it. It always seemed to revolve around her telling me off, saying I hadn't done my maths properly. Samantha's persona took the form of an extremely strict teacher who frequently made me cry. I was an easy target, of course – I hadn't even started school yet!

When we played shops, we'd take tins out of Mum's kitchen cupboards, and tubes of toothpaste from the bathroom, balancing all of our stock on top of a wicker linen basket. It lived on the landing at the top of the stairs, where it was ideally placed for receiving reluctant customers on their way to the toilet. On top of the basket we'd place a plastic till, which we were both desperate to operate. Whoever got to the shower cap first could transform themselves into the shopkeeper by pulling it over their head. This shop uniform made us feel very professional!

Samantha and I didn't play together for as many years as I'd have liked, simply because she was six years older than I, and soon tired of my childish antics. But what really brought the whole thing to a premature end was something I did to her, which I still feel bad about even now. I stole her only worldly friend away from her. Natalie had been a lifeline for Samantha, connecting her to the world outside of the Fellowship. For many of us, those links kept us sane. I think it broke her heart, and I don't think she ever forgave me for that.

From then on, I felt as if I were the only child in the house. While she became more reserved, I busied myself with my worldly friends. My brother and sisters were growing up fast, but I still had a lot of playing to do.

There's a lot I don't know about my brother, Victor. He'd spent twelve years finding his feet in the male-dominated world of the Fellowship even before I was born. He was two years old when the Fellowship split into opposing subgroups, Mum and Dad ending up in the more extreme of the two, and my mum's parents totally cut off from us in the other. Victor lived through all that, growing up in the 1970s. I know it all affected him greatly, but it didn't stop him loving and treating me like his baby. And those twelve years that separated us might as well have been twelve minutes for all the difference they made to our relationship.

I really loved my big brother. I followed him everywhere and couldn't wait for him to wake up in the morning. I listened out for his call for me as soon as his alarm went off and delighted in acting as his slave. On request, I brought him cups of coffee and ferried messages back and forth between him and Mum. She was much too busy to bother about my brother when he was lazing in bed, but that was OK by me.

I loved it when Victor helped me with projects. One time I designed a set of heart-shaped shelves, which he assisted me in making. Whatever I wanted, he'd find a way of incorporating it into his own woodwork projects during his apprenticeship as a carpenter. As was usual practice in the Fellowship, he left school at sixteen, skipping his A-levels and learning a practical trade.

Victor was really handy with a can of paint, and sometimes Dad entrusted him with it to touch up the rusty spots on his Fiat Panorama. Dad didn't believe in spending money on new cars until he had run his current one into the ground. By the time he had finished with it, the bodywork would be more Polyfilla than metal. The Panorama was an estate car, which carted the six of us around, four in the front and two in the luggage compartment, hanging on for dear life. I was rather glad when the law for wearing seat belts in the backs of cars was enforced a few years later.

Victor may have been handy with a spray can, but he couldn't really be trusted with one. It always started off all right, then, having finished the job in hand, he looked round for more things to spray. On this particular occasion it was my tricycle that he turned to. I loved that little trike and whizzed around at top speed on it, leaning around the corners with one wheel off the ground. One day I dashed into the garage to grab it and, on seeing it, burst into floods of tears. Across the front of this dear little red trike was a spray mark of blue paint. It wasn't a big mark, about the size of my four-year-old palm, but to me the blemish was the end of the world. I had no doubt in my mind who was responsible for this horrible stain.

'Victor,' I howled, 'look what you've done!'

He popped his head out of the shed, a sheepish look on his face. 'Sorry, Lindsey,' he grinned. My anguish drained away at the sight of him, and immediately I forgave him. But I could never ride that tricycle again with quite the same pride. I got used to Victor's destructiveness, though. I had to. He didn't think twice about cutting my doll's hair, and once even found he had crushed some of my toy cars in the vice that lived in the shed. He claimed they had been in a car crash.

When I was about nine, I asked Victor to take me out. What I really wanted was for him to take me fishing with him. He regarded me with a funny look on his face and said he wasn't sure. I realized then that he was embarrassed by me. I wore clothes that didn't fit in with the other girls my age and he clearly minded this detail. I was hurt by his embarrassment, and never asked him again. As I grew older, our relationship changed, and for a time we grew apart, but eventually events would bring us closer together again.

Chapter Five

Motherly Love

In one very particular way, I was a normal child. I was inquisitive, and wanted to know 'why?' all the time. Unfortunately, most of my questions, which I put to my mum and dad, were met with the same unsatisfying response: 'Let the Lord into your heart and have faith,' they would say. In other words, don't ask questions. They might as well have been saying, 'Don't be Lindsey.'

One day I was in the kitchen helping Mum bake, when a question popped into my head.

'How is God going to win the war against the Devil if there are more worldly people than Fellowship people?' I mumbled through a mouthful of cake mixture.

'Trust the Lord, Lindsey, He knows what He's doing. And it's very naughty to question Him.'

With no further questions, I carried on licking the spoon.

I wasn't allowed to do sponsored charity events at school, so another time I asked, 'Mum, how come we don't give to money to charities that help people?'

'That's not what God has chosen us to do,' Mum simply said. 'There are other people to look after the poor.'

Being told that God had all the answers and there was no point trying to work anything out for myself was supposed to stop me asking questions. The problem was that it just gave me a great idea. If God had all the answers, I could ask Him. 'Dear God, what am I getting for my birthday this year?' I whispered, so Mum couldn't hear me. She was standing at the foot of the beds making sure we said our prayers properly.

'In the name of the Lord Jesus Christ, Amen.' I waited for my answer.

As far as Mum was concerned, all my questions about the ways of the world were unimportant. The Bible dealt with those completely and that was all there was to it. As I think she probably saw it, my questioning was just a minor diversion from the really important things in life. These were practical everyday things, such as baking and knitting. In a way, she was right. We had a great time together. Mum loved to buy *Family Circle*, a magazine for mums, full of arts-and-crafts ideas. She'd keep the best ideas in a folder and, when she'd finished all her jobs, we'd get out the paints, glue, glitter and scissors and get to work.

Mum also kept huge bags containing scraps of material and wool, which we used to make a collage man on one occasion. She drew the outline on a huge piece of paper and I stuck on wool for hair, buttons for eyes and various patches of cloth to make the clothes. She taught me to knit and sew, and we made clothes for my dolls.

When we weren't doing arts and crafts we were either playing board games or heading out to the shops. It might not sound exciting, but I really enjoyed shopping with Mum, especially if we passed the post office with the cakes in the window. (It's amazing how hungry you feel after posting a letter.) Bizarrely, it had a sweet counter at one end and a bakery at the other. I wasn't so interested in the sweets, but Mum and I would make sure that we never went home without my cream bun and her horseshoe-shaped macaroon.

Two shops down from cake heaven was the hardware shop. Mum did a lot of practical jobs around the house, so we would often pop in there for one or two items on the way to the post office. One day, while she scoured the shelves for the things on her list, I waited at the front of the shop, watching as the man behind the counter measured out nails and hooks and weighed them on his scales. I was fascinated by the huge cast-iron weighing scales, which put Mum's home set to shame. It was then that I noticed that the television fixed on the wall was on. I had seen televisions before but I had never had the chance to see one that was switched on. I looked up curiously.

There were some strange creatures dancing around in front of a row of houses. Popping out of the dustbin next to the steps was a shaggy-looking thing that was clearly neither a human nor an animal. I had no idea what I was seeing. I'd never seen anything like it before, but even so I was far more interested in getting off home with Mum and eating cake. That, not TV, was what was missing from my life at that moment in time.

I had some really nice times with Mum.

If Mum had to go to the doctor's, or anywhere that involved a lot of waiting around, my grandma would take care of me for a few hours. Gladys was my dad's mum, and she and my grandpa lived just a couple of minutes away by car. They rented a large Victorian terraced house from Uncle Hubert, who was married to my dad's sister, Meryl. We'd always have to park in the multi-storey car park built directly behind the terrace, from where we could see Grandma if she was near her kitchen window. If she was looking out, I'd wave, and she'd be waiting at the front door by the time we got there.

I'd head straight out to the shed, which took up most of the tiny back garden and was used as a sewing room. I would sit at the old Singer sewing machine that stood just inside the doorway, thumping my foot on the treadle. I liked to pretend I was making clothes the way I saw Mum and Alice do.

Sometimes I'd see the stray cats that Grandma encouraged to come into her garden by leaving bowls of milk and scraps of food for them. I thought this was pretty daring, because Fellowship members were not allowed to keep pets, just in case they came to love them more than God. Maybe that rule was created just for Grandma, because she certainly loved them. Whenever we exchanged letters, hers would always tell me about the latest cats visiting her garden, and in my letters back to her I'd try to please her by drawing pictures of the ones she described.

I'd always hand my letters directly to Grandma when I saw her at the meetings. After the meeting was over, and everyone had gone outside, I'd run along the rows of benches to where Grandma was usually sitting, waiting for me. I'd tug her long plait of white hair and she'd creak round with a big smile on her face. I was always excited to have another letter for her. I'd ask when I could visit her, hoping to get my foot pumping on that treadle again. If my cousins, Hubert's boys, were doing something at the house, she'd say, 'Not this week, Lindsey, I've got the boys in.' She loved her boys, possibly almost as much as she loved her cats.

The same can't be said for Grandpa, who hated cats. Maybe he was afraid she'd love them more than him. Such was his dislike of them that there was a family legend involving him, a cat and a kitchen door. We all knew the story, but the truth of it was never confirmed. Apparently, he once caught a trespassing cat inside the house, and furiously slammed the door on it as it tried to escape. It was a horrible image and I didn't want to think of Grandpa doing that.

One of the rooms upstairs in Grandma's house was Grandpa's office. He was always up there doing something, so if I was visiting I'd hardly get to see him at all. I'd often go up to a back bedroom to get a book for Grandma to read to me, and would pop my head round the door as I passed Grandpa's office. He always seemed to be sitting at his desk with his back to the door. He wasn't one for showing much affection, but if I went in he'd always stop what he was doing and invite me to choose a coloured sticker from the top drawer of his desk. In retrospect, I think they must have been items of office stationery, but I thought they were there just for me.

I particularly liked to be allowed to stay for lunch. Grandma's special was crinkle-cut oven chips with dollops of ketchup. We just had the straight kind of chips at home, so I thought the fancy-shaped ones were wonderful. When it was time for lunch it was my job to run and sound the gong that hung from the ceiling in the hallway. This was Grandpa's cue to put his stickers away and come downstairs.

After lunch I'd go upstairs to Grandma's room to have a sleep on her big bouncy bed. It was covered with a large green eiderdown, which was so slippery that I had a job just getting on the bed in the first place. She'd lie down together with me and we'd cuddle up. At some point in the afternoon, Mum would arrive to pick me up. Mum never hung around to chat to Grandma, and I suspect they may not have got on too well, but to me she was special.

Chapter Six

The Ministry

Every month a package would arrive, delivered by a member of the Fellowship. This contained the books that told my parents how to live their lives. These were the Ministry, and we had accumulated hundreds of them. Victor's carpentry skills were called into action by Dad, who got him to build several enormous sets of shelves and attach them to the walls on either side of the chimney breast in our dining room. They were completely filled with the volumes of the Ministry. Red books, green books, brown books, white books … I loved looking at the colours, but I wasn't interested in what was in them. Mum and Dad would read every word, process the information and then tell me how a Fellowship girl was expected to behave.

Sometimes I went with Dad, and a few other Fellowship men, to the High Street to do some preaching. Everyone would stand with their back to the glass front of the local Woolworth's store, while the men took it in turn to step forward to preach. No one ever came out of Woolworth's to tell us to 'piss off', so we must have had some sort of pitch licence.

When it was Dad's turn, he would step forward into the bustling crowd with confidence and begin to read from the Bible earnestly. The thing I loved about Dad was that he seemed completely unbothered by the crowd. His confidence gave me confidence to be there; he made it seem like something to be proud of.

Most people just ignored us, but Dad carried on as if he had a captive audience. This happened once a month on a Saturday, when the high street was busy and there were no meetings to go, and it was the only time the Fellowship spoke publicly. I'm not sure if we were supposed to be converting sinners, but, if we were, it was a dismal failure. The only attention I remember getting was from the driver of a speeding white van, who slowed down just enough to shout out a volley of blasphemous abuse at us, before whizzing off in fits of laughter. Well, at least he showed some interest.

Reading all those ministry books and endless chapters from the Bible got tedious, even for Dad, so the reading of the daily broadsheet was a real treat for him in the evenings. Before starting he made sure he had everything he'd need to sustain him throughout the evening. First, he'd carefully snip the corner off a packet of peanuts and lean it against the leg of his favourite chair where he sat, so that they were within arm's reach. This allowed him to slide his hand down and grab the packet without taking his eyes from the page. Nearby, he'd place a glass of sherry, which could also be located without looking.

Very carefully he aligned the pages of the paper, making sure he had the large cumbersome sheets under strict control. When everything was in order, he'd settle back in the armchair and balance the newspaper on his knees. Between regular munches of peanuts and sips of sherry, he gave sharp twitches of his head and nods of approval. If he got really involved in an article, he'd let out sharp lisping noises: the sound of him muttering under his breath. Victor and I found Dad's habits hilariously funny. Without a TV, watching Dad was our evening's entertainment.

Sometimes, he'd let out roars of laughter, calling out, 'Edith, have you seen this?' to which Mum would retort sharply, while her knitting needles clattered away, 'Of course not, Peter, I've been far too busy.'

Eventually, Dad's head would slump onto his chest and he'd begin snoring. This was our chance! Very carefully, one of us would begin to slide the paper from between his fingers. As soon as he felt the precious *Telegraph* slipping from his grasp, his head would snap up, and he'd shout, 'I was reading that!' and our chance was gone. And, of course, there wasn't a hope in hell of taking away from Dad what was his only window on the world beyond the Fellowship.

Chapter Seven

School of Thought

When I was five I started my first year at the local primary school. At long last I was a big girl. I was particularly proud to be at the very same school my dad had attended when he was a lad. What's more, I was following in the footsteps of Alice, Victor and Samantha. I couldn't wait to let everyone in my class know that I had a big sister in the junior school. And I felt so important, putting on my best dress and shoes.

Samantha relished her big sister role, telling me which teachers to watch out for and what I could expect to encounter.

'You're lucky you won't have Mrs Cook,' she told me, enigmatically.

I wasn't sure why this was meant to be lucky, but I nodded gravely. I accepted that Mrs Cook was capable of terrible things.

'Your teacher,' Samantha revealed, 'is called Mrs Roland.' Samantha had heard good things about Mrs Roland. Nothing terrible, anyway.

'I'm going to call her Roland Rat,' I announced. I had a sticker of Roland Rat attached to the headboard of my bed, so he meant a lot to me.

'No, Lindsey, you don't want to do that,' she warned.

'Yes, I do,' I said defiantly, but I wisely never said it to Mrs Roland's face.

Pretty soon, though, on the first morning, I was sitting in that Welfare office on the plastic chair, with all the Asian children. No one in the family prepared me for that.

The only preparation for school I was given by my parents was intended to make sure I followed the Fellowship rules while there. How I coped with that in the school environment was left up to me.

It was when I started school that I began to realize how my life really differed from those of the rest of my friends. I didn't want to stand out, but having to follow the Fellowship's rules made it difficult not to.

One of the first friends I made at primary school was Catherine. I can't remember much about her now, but I must have thought she was nice, because I invited her back to my house. For some reason I decided that the Fellowship rule of not having worldly people in the house wouldn't apply on that day. I was living in the moment and it seemed right. I was only five.

Mum was busy helping Alice make her wedding dress that day and had asked Catherine's mum if she could walk me to the corner of Albion Avenue on the way home, to make sure I arrived safely. But when it came to saying goodbye I found myself asking, 'Can Catherine come to my house and play?'

Catherine's mum sounded unsure. 'I don't think we can, Lindsey, that's not … I don't think we're allowed to do that.' But there was no stopping me now.

'It's going to be fine,' I said.

Together all three of us headed up Albion Avenue, right to my front door.

When Mum opened the door her face said it all. The two adults looked each other: Mum in her sensible skirt and blouse, and Catherine's mum in her bright-pink leg warmers. I don't know who was more embarrassed. I had done wrong.

'I'm sorry,' Mum managed to say to Catherine and her mum … I pushed past her and ran into the front room. Alice was kneeling on the floor, surrounded by acres of material. I looked at all that white satin and in a moment I had forgotten my bad deed. After Mum had dispatched Catherine, she entered the room, picked up the scissors and carried on cutting carefully around the edges of the wedding-dress pattern. She didn't say a word.

I did not invite my school friends home again.

Halfway through my first day at primary school, I came across a problem. Most of the other children were having packed lunch or cooked dinner at school, whereas I was expected to go home. I really didn't want to be the odd one out, so I looked for somewhere to hide.

Off to the side of our classroom was a long cloakroom with benches down the middle and our coat pegs on the walls. It seemed like the perfect place, so I ducked behind the door and hoped no one would find me. Samantha somehow knew I'd be there, and took me home straightaway.

I soon found out that going home for lunch wasn't the problem for me: it was coming back afterwards. By the time I returned, everyone would be playing out in the field and playground. Even worse was when it was raining and all the pupils were inside the hall, sitting at tables laden with various arts, crafts and games. I'd arrive at the hall doors, and look through the panes of glass at everyone busy in their groups, working away at their activities. Taking a breath, I'd push the doors open, and, with a bright smile on my face, walk in.

I always had the fear that everyone would stop what they were doing and look at me, seeing how different I was. In fact, no one really noticed, but every day the fear was the same. In the playground I would try to join the groups and games, kick a ball around, play on the cement blocks or on the climbing frame. The need to blend in was everything to me. I was proud to be part of the Fellowship, but that was of no value with my friends and offered me no protection among them.

I managed to fit in most of the time. I may have had to wear ribbons in my hair, but that was nothing out of the ordinary for a young girl. And our school uniform was a blessing for me. I could wear the requisite grey skirt (keeping it below my knees, of course), without breaking Fellowship rules. Most of the time it was just the school assembly and lunch that caused me problems, but I was disappointed not to be allowed to join after-school clubs. I couldn't go to Brownies, or swimming, or join a book club. Generally speaking, if it had the word 'club' in the title, I wasn't allowed to attend. Luckily, though, the person who started the after-school netball didn't call it a club, preferring the word 'team'. Well done to them, because I was allowed to play as goal attack and competed against other schools. I loved it and was even made captain, but it was a short-lived affair. My parents eventually decided to crack down on teams too, just to be on the safe side.

In my first year at school, a boy in my class handed out party invitations, one of which was addressed to me. I felt no joy, though. Instead, I knew immediately that it was another situation highlighting the fact that I couldn't be normal and go to a party. I was saved from having to make my excuses by one of the other girls in the class shouting out, 'Oh, don't give an invitation to Lindsey. She doesn't go to parties.'

I certainly didn't thank her for that, though. It was a bad situation made a billion times worse by her loud mouth.

I made sure I had plenty of friends at school, but I was always looking for ways to prove myself to them. If I had to be different it would be on my terms; I wanted my differences to be envied rather than thought odd. I was very proud of my muscles and started defining myself by how strong I was. I once carried Yvonne Worthington on my back down to the bottom of the playing field and back up again to prove my brawn. Yvonne was extraordinarily tall, towering above everyone else, so she was the obvious target.

Once, I started a fire in the grounds of the school. I was out to impress the kids in the street, and creating a blaze on council property seemed as good a way as any to do that.

We'd somehow managed to lay our hands on a box of matches and soon people were challenging each other to see who would dare to light a fire. Of course, I put my hand up. No one thought I'd have the guts to do it, but I climbed over the gate, as I regularly did for a bit of excitement, and stood on the drive in full view of the road and school caretaker's office.

I collected up some leaves and twigs, plonked them on the tarmac and shoved a match under the driest-looking twig. To my horror it caught fire. I started stamping on the flames with my rubber-soled shoes. I was really scared at that point

– not about burning my foot though: I feared that my parents would notice the charring on my shoe. The fire eventually went out but my shoes were blackened. I scraped them the best I could and hoped for the best. They never found out.

Another time I was in the school grounds again, throwing stones. One of my shots whizzed over the gate and hit a car parked outside on the road. There was a loud bang. I ran to see what I had done, excited and horrified. I saw where my stone had landed and I saw a dent in one of the cars.

I always took it too far – that was the thing. I was always so keen to impress people. I can see now it was just my way of finding an outlet. My life was restricted in so many ways that my antics were inevitable. It seemed to me that the other kids didn't feel the same need to light fires, throw stones or trespass. They were quite happy watching TV.

I think I got away with a lot more than many other Fellowship children did. I was always allowed to play out in the street with worldly children, as long as I didn't try to take them home, and, after my experience with Catherine, I wasn't planning to try that again.

From the day I heard about the school trip I began to dread the time when we were asked if we wanted to go. It was an exciting week-long outing that happened in our last year, and all the children were taken to Wales to stay in a hostel. I'd heard about how they all had wonderful adventures together. I was dreading it – I knew I would have to stay at home and attend school without my friends.

Mum sent me to school clutching the permission request slip, stating that I was not allowed on the trip. I handed it to my teacher, Mrs Renowlden, and sat down at my desk in the middle of the classroom. She leafed through the slips of paper checking each one and then made her way over to see me. Without speaking, she crouched down beside me so that her face was level with mine.

'Lindsey,' she said quietly. 'Your parents won't let you to go on the school trip, is that right?'

I nodded. I was mortified but I wasn't going to show it.

'Is it because of religious reasons, or because of ... money?'

I considered what my teacher was asking. My family weren't rich, but we lived in a nice house and I had all the toys I wanted. In that respect my parents were pretty generous with their money. The money that I was allowed to drop into the collection bowl at the meetings seemed to me to be an enormous amount.

Of course, I knew what the reason was. If I went on the trip I would be exposed to all kinds of evil and would have to eat with worldly people. That was definitely not allowed. Somehow I knew my kindly teacher would find this difficult to understand, and I didn't want to talk about it in front of the class.

'Money,' I lied.

When I was with other Fellowship children I had nothing to hide because we were all alike. From the age of five, I found myself in situations where I had to deal with a school full of people, who knew I was not at all like them. Very early on, I decided to minimize my apparent differences, and do my best to hide them.

My friend Kerry lived a few doors down from me. She was a year younger and much smaller, which had its advantages when we were role-playing mother and baby. She was always doing back flips and handstands and cartwheels on her garden lawn and was the ideal build for a gymnast. To me, she was a show-off, but I didn't let her know I had such terrible thoughts because then I wouldn't have access to her fantastic collection of toys!

The only problem was, Kerry wouldn't let me play with her toys most of the time. I thought she was really selfish. It didn't occur to me that I hadn't invited her into my house to play with my toys.

I badgered her to let me ride her plastic tractor, and pleaded to have a play with the old-fashioned sprung pram with huge wheels, which lived in her shed. If I was lucky I could strike a deal with her. She'd let me push her pram if she could pretend to be my baby and sit inside. I'd wheel her up and down the pavement, both of us thinking that we were convincing the passing neighbours that she was my offspring.

I may have had a beautiful piano at home but what I didn't have was an organ with two keyboards, stops and bass pedals. How I wished Kerry would let me have a go on it. If worse came to worst, and I wasn't given access to the toys, I'd sit on the organ stool silently banging away at the keys, pretending it was switched on. It was torture for me. They had all this great stuff and no idea how frustrating I felt not be able to play with it.

Kerry had a great garden with a shed at the bottom where all the best toys were kept, together with the pram and the tractor. As soon as I got to her house, I'd make a beeline for that shed.

One day I was at Kerry's house playing with dolls in the conservatory at the back of the house. This involved a lot of undressing and dressing them in a variety of splendid outfits. It was while we were doing this that we noticed that they didn't have any privates. How did they wee and poo? we wondered. We needed to do some research on this, so Kerry, her older sister Felicity and I all took off our knickers and started comparing parts.

When Kerry's mum walked in to offer us some orange squash and biscuits, she found us all sitting there with skirts hitched up, bare-bummed. Bizarrely enough, for the only Fellowship girl in the room, I didn't feel we had done anything wrong. We were just looking at our bits. But Kerry's mother was very strict and she sent me home. Her reaction seemed a bit extreme and I didn't understand why she made a fuss. But the main reason I was upset was that it threatened my friendship with Kerry. If her door was closed to me, that would mean no more playing with her pram, tractor and organ.

After that day I would often see Kerry playing in her garden behind her high, wooden gate, and sometimes I got up the courage to knock on her door.

'No,' her mum would tell me, again and again, 'Kerry can't play with you today.'

Chapter Eight

Trouble with the Neighbours

I suppose my street was typical of many of the calm suburban roads beyond the chaos of the town centre. The trees that lined the pavements were useful to us children for hiding behind when tracking intruders on our territory, and provided an invaluable supply of sticks we used for whacking each other.

I knew most of the neighbours, but of particular interest to me was Jim, who lived in the house opposite ours and had the largest front garden in the street. Jim was a war veteran and it was widely known that he had spent time in Japanese prisoner-of-war camps. This piece of information was passed between the neighbours, with knowing looks from the adults and unsympathetic sniggers from the kids. He was an easy target for us merciless children. With shouts of rage he defended his land and primly painted bungalow against any child or adult who so much as dared to stroll past the white picket fence that controlled the border between friend and foe.

He had almost met his match in me, though. I could also be fiercely defensive. I had good reason to defend my family, I thought. They would not defend themselves as they staunchly avoided confrontation. Having watched Jim reverse his car into Mum's one day, without so much as a look at the damage, and witnessed him pouring bricks from a wheelbarrow over Mum's feet, I decided it was time for revenge.

Gathering up as many of my friends as I could find playing out that evening, I laid the plans for the battle. Carefully splitting off the sturdy stems of Jim's roses, we armed ourselves with rosehips and scuttled back to the protection of the cars parked opposite his house. One by one we ran across the road and flung those hard missiles at his windows. Time and again we watched the lights in his house go on and the curtains pull back. The thrill was superb. And then it was halted abruptly. We had been seen.

'Lindsey! Come in, *now!*' Mum bellowed.

One of the neighbours, Kathy, had rung my mum to say that her daughter was causing trouble.

Game over.

Legitimate revenge was never far away, though. For most people Sunday is a day of rest. But for Jim. Poor old Jim! That was the day that the Fellowship descended on Albion Avenue. Cars casually pulled up onto the kerb outside his bungalow and helplessly he looked on while a procession of men, accompanied by their long-skirted wives, ambled across the road and into our house, from where I watched Jim with a warm glow of satisfaction. Even *he* could not defend himself against *us*.

A new rule had come in that said all Fellowship families should, if possible, move to a house that was not joined to any other. But Mum and Dad could not afford to move, so we stayed where we were. Sometimes I thanked my lucky stars that I lived in a semi-detached house.

One evening a sound snaked its way through the walls of our neighbour Kathy's house and into our front room, where I was sitting with Mum and Dad.

Thump-thump-thump-chukka-chukka.

My ears pricked up, excitedly. Mum carried on with her knitting, but Dad looked up from his paper towards the wall and tutted.

Thump-thump-thump-chukka-chukka.

I quickly got up and went into the kitchen. I knew what to do. I took a glass from the cupboard and crept into the dining room, where no one could see what I was doing, then pressed the container up against the wall. There it was again, but clearer now.

Thump-thump-thump-chukka-chukka.

For a brief moment I let the forbidden music pass through the crude amplifier into my ear and felt good. Then I pulled away.

Returning to the front room to do what I thought was right. I took down the horn that hung from a corner of a shelf.

Thoooooooot! Thoooooooot!

I blew as hard as I could.

Thoooooooot! Thoooooooot!

I had let the Devil into my soul and now I had to drown him out. After a minute or two, Mum and Dad expressed their objection to my awful racket.

But I had done it. I had resisted the temptation of evil and felt proud.

Satan was not coming into our house.

Perhaps the Fellowship was right to be cautious about living at such close proximity to the Devil.

Chapter Nine

Bound by the Rules

We all took it in turns to have Fellowship members to our homes on Sundays for a meal. Sometimes we had to have them after the morning meetings for the 'Break'. I really liked the 'Breaks'. Sausage rolls, crisps and sandwiches would come out on trays, like a kind of buffet. The other kids and I would run around stuffing food in our mouths as we played. I especially liked the evening meal. If it was Mum's turn we would arrive home from the last meeting of the day and open the front door to the smell of meat and potatoes roasting in the oven that Mum had left on using the timer. Then it was a rush to get the table laid for ten or twelve visitors.

Mum used the best cutlery. It lived in a wooden canteen that Mum and Dad had received as a wedding present in the 1960s. I loved to open the lid and look at the dull shine of the stainless steel. I hoped that one day Mum would give it to me so that I could feel proud when I entertained the Fellowship.

My place would be set at a little trolley on wheels. If I was lucky, the visitors would have kids, and we would mess around the whole evening while the adults talked endlessly. More often than not, I ended up lying across Mum's knee, exhausted. I'd drift off to sleep in that position, feeling secure with the drone of voices washing over me.

Mum and Dad groaned when we were told it was our turn to go to the Walkers' house for dinner and we went with a feeling of dread. Once, a Fellowship member visiting the Walkers for lunch had found a hair in his cup of tea. This news had spread like wildfire through the Fellowship and now no one wanted to go to their house. It did not help that all the family had greasy-looking black hair – it wasn't even as if the hair in the cup of tea would be clean!

So when I heard that Colin Walker was coming to live with us I was mortified.

This was my first experience of Fellowship members being 'shut up'.

I had heard that it was a terrible thing, but I couldn't see why. If it meant that Fellowship members came to stay at our house, well that was exciting to me. Victor's bed was replaced with bunk beds, which were squeezed into his tiny room. Our house was buzzing with anticipation. We'd never had anyone to stay before. Colin arrived with one suitcase and was grinning madly. To me, a four-year-old, he looked like a huge gangly stick insect, with the Walker mop of black greasy hair on top. I soon grew to love having Colin around and forgot to check for greasy black hairs in our tea cups. From then on, my games became even more adventurous. I had two brothers to tease.

Colin had an obsession with lawn mowers and would bring them home to dismantle in the back garden. Mum was furious about it. The garden was her territory, and here he was, spilling oil and leaving rusty engines all over the lawn. He'd work away out there for hours, but we never really knew what he was doing. The lawn mowers never seemed to work.

The strange thing was that Colin's mum, dad and sister never came to visit. And they lived only a few streets away. When I asked Mum why no one came to see Colin she explained the big secret. She told me that his sister, Lois, had 'given in to temptation'. I was too young to be told what she'd done, but I could tell it was a serious matter.

Colin's family stopped coming to the meetings and no one in the Fellowship saw them. Colin was old enough to leave home, and free of sin, so he was encouraged to go to a Fellowship household that hadn't been touched by the Devil.

Then, after a few months, as suddenly as he had arrived, Colin moved out and everything returned to normal. Apparently, Lois had left home, taking her sins with her.

I never thought anything like this would happen to us.

After Colin left, we went back to visiting the Walkers every so often for dinner, but Lois was never mentioned again.

I was just glad that my own sisters were still around.

Being so much older, Alice was almost motherly towards me and treated me like a baby doll. One day she said she was going shopping in the town and asked if I wanted anything. I said, immediately, 'The star-shaped transforming figure.' I had seen it on the toy pages of the Argos catalogue. It was a solid plastic device in light lilac and I thought it would change my life. I waited impatiently for her to come home and almost wet myself with excitement. At last she appeared and, with a flourish, produced a package for me. My heart sank. Where was the cardboard box? What she handed to me was a soft tissue-wrapped parcel, which I opened. Out fell a pair of suede, fake-fur-lined mittens. Oh, the disappointment!

Shortly after the mitten incident Alice married her childhood sweetheart, Mike Edmonds. She left the house crying her eyes out. What was all the fuss? I wondered. She was only moving round the corner! She drove off with her new husband in his car, dragging the tin cans behind it that had been tied on by my brother and his friends. White clouds of shaving foam drifted into the air, ruining the carefully sprayed message 'Good Luck!' It was a time of great celebration and joy in our house.

Such joy.

It's hard to remember when I first noticed a change in our house. Certainly for the first few weeks after Alice left I was still reeling with excitement. Now I had to share a room with only one sister and had a new house to visit. Alice seemed a little reluctant to let me come and mess up her nice new house, but it was arranged that I would have breakfast with her, one Sunday morning, after the Supper. I couldn't wait!

Well I was in for a shock. At home we ate our cereal first, then hot stuff, such as baked beans on toast, or fishcakes. I sat down at Alice's table and waited for my breakfast to arrive. She wasted time asking me how everyone was at home and if I was missing her. I just wished she'd hurry up; I was starving. Finally she brought it out and I grabbed my spoon in readiness.

What!

Where was my cereal? In front of me was a plate. Not a bowl, but a plate! I looked at the crisp slice of toast dripping with butter and honey.

It wasn't right at all, but I was so tempted. Pushing my confusion aside I stuffed the warm food in my mouth. Mmmm. Crisp on the outside and light and fluffy on the inside. Just how I liked it.

Alice may not do things the same way as Mum, but she knew how to make good toast!

I wish I hadn't cared so much about that toast and had told her that I missed her. But I didn't know then that I wouldn't see her again for a very long time.

As a six-year-old, I wasn't told what was going on. I just had a sense that things were not quite right in our house. What happened was discussed by a committee of male priests behind closed doors. But what I can say is this.

Radio and recorded music, which might expose us to worldly influences, were banned, so the first job my dad did when he bought a car was take out the radio-cassette player and store it away in a drawer, to put back in if he ever sold the vehicle. My brother was not like my dad. He bought a Fiat Strada when he was eighteen and didn't remove the radio. He just wanted to do what other teenagers did. Someone in the Fellowship noticed and accusations of sinful behaviour were made. Mum looked under Victor's bed, found some music cassettes and threw them out.

If only that had been the end of it, but it wasn't. There were further accusations, including something about a deliberate car crash outside a meeting room, and a trip to the cinema. I don't know what was true and what was not, but it didn't really matter. Mum and Dad thought that the priests were just looking for a reason to punish them, and Victor was the scapegoat. Mum and Dad were considered trouble-makers themselves, speaking up about things they thought were corrupt. It didn't pay to question those in charge.

At the last meeting I ever went to, I stood outside in the car park with my friend Stelly – two little girls in their best dresses and matching headscarves among the hundred or so cars. We did not rush about as we usually did. I looked at her. She was perfect: a good Fellowship girl.

'It's going to happen, isn't it?' I asked.

'Lindsey, you are not going to be "shut up",' she replied. 'You're just not.'

She sounded so sure.

I never saw her again.

'Bastards!' Samantha shouted. We were supposed to be in bed but the pair of us were sitting at the top of the stairs, leaning forward, craning our necks to peek down through the gaps in the banisters and get a good look into the hallway. Her profanity must have been heard, but no one looked up.

We watched two men being ushered into our front room. Through the open door we saw Mum and Victor rise to greet them, then Dad shut the door firmly behind them. There was nothing more to see, so Samantha and I returned to our bedroom. Unusually for me I asked if I could get into her bed. She sounded glad that I'd asked. I got in under her bedcovers and snuggled up against her warm, soft body.

I felt so scared. I had a terrible feeling inside.

Mum knitted cardigans, booties, and bonnets in readiness for the birth of Alice's first baby. I watched her place them side by side on her bed and I admired the soft white woollen garments. She wrapped them in tissue paper and carefully packed them away in a shoe box. This was a symbol of hope: we would be returning to our rightful place in Fellowship any day now, and the present was ready for that day. We waited for the call to come.

On Monday morning I got up and went to school as usual. I did my school work and played with all my friends. When I got home the house seemed changed in some way. Mum wasn't rushing around trying to get the dinner on the table. When Dad burst through the door he wasn't complaining about the terrible traffic on the M25. We ate our dinner calmly. And Dad did not leave the house.

The day after, it was the same. The phone didn't ring. Again, we ate our dinner calmly. And again Dad did not leave the house.

Days turned into weeks and weeks into months.

'Why is this happening to us?' Mum asked no one in particular, over and over again. We were now 'shut up', so there was no one to answer her.

Victor left home. He handed me and Samantha £200 each. It seemed as if he was going away for ever. When Lois left her family they were let back into the Fellowship. But this didn't happen to us.

We didn't know when Victor was coming back, so Mum said I could have his room. Now I had one all to myself! Mum stripped off the hideous classic-cars wallpaper and put up something more to my taste – something girly. I painted pictures of flowers on the chest of drawers and hung my 'Pears Soap' poster on the wall. It didn't take me long to settle in!

Alice was still our family and we loved her dearly. But now she was married she had her own household – one that was free from sin.

There was no argument. No fuss. No one made anyone do what they did. Barbed-wire fences and padlocked gates were not put up around our home. And there was always the phone. But that was the end of our relationship with Alice. In fact, it was the end of our relationship with everyone in the Fellowship. No telephone calls, no Sunday dinner with other families. No meetings. It was just the way things were done. These were the rules and the rules were everything. Mum and Dad just accepted them.

And so did I – for a while.

It took me three long years, a third of my life, to work up the courage to make contact with Alice again.

One sunny afternoon, I came home from school to an empty house. Mum worked now. We needed the money and she needed the company of other adults. She had a job at the local hospital, working in medical records, and that was how she'd found out about the birth of Alice's first baby.

No one told us. It was as if we no longer existed.

The news of the baby started me thinking about what Alice's life might be like. I fantasized about finding her. She'd give me a big cuddle and say it was all over. God had sorted it out and we were welcomed back.

In the empty house, I picked up the phone. My heart was thumping. I had found her number in the directory a few days before and already had it scribbled down on a scrap of paper, hidden at the back of a drawer. A guilty secret.

I dialled the number.

Brrr-brrr, brrr-brrr, it purred.

I almost put the phone down. What was I doing? I began to feel God's eyes looking directly at me.

'Hello?' a woman's voice said. It was her, my sister.

'Hello,' I replied. 'It's me.'

'Who?'

'Me, Lindsey.'

There was a moment of silence. 'Do you want to speak to the priests?'

The police? I thought. Does she want me to speak to the police? I'd made a big mistake. I put the phone down and never told anyone about what I'd done. I'd sinned. That night I prayed for forgiveness.

I'd never knowingly heard the word 'priests' before. I had no idea what it meant. When I did hear it again, I froze. All of a sudden I really wanted to know what a priest was.

Victor had also become a distant figure. It was just the four of us now, living in our little bubble, between worlds.

The waiting brought out the nervousness in Dad. He didn't rush about, but he'd twitch annoyingly, a lot of the time. He'd often pace about, fingers clenched together behind his back. His long legs and straight back took his broad, shiny, bald head somewhere over six feet. From up there, he'd loom over Mum, hoping to grab a rare cuddle.

Mum wasn't always very affectionate, but her face was built for smiling and that helped her get along with the worldly people she worked with. She could chat away for hours with anyone, given the chance. Dad was friendly, too, but his unrest made it harder for him to let go. He was happier discussing practical matters, like the traffic and work. He was an authority on organization, which suited his clear, strong voice. Mum spoke well, too, but, like both Victor's and mine, her north London accent became more apparent when she was chatting excitedly.

Samantha was a mixture of the two: soft and cuddly like Mum, but tall like Dad, with a large broad face. When she grinned, it was so complete that her eyes would almost disappear. She'd look at people secretly without turning her head, taking everything in from the corner of her eye.

When it became clear to the Fellowship that Mum and Dad were not going to repent for Victor's sins they were 'withdrawn from'. This is the ultimate rejection by the Fellowship, from which there is no return. Mum and Dad had taken Victor's sins upon themselves by refusing to believe that he had done anything wrong.

The Fellowship may have abandoned us but there was no way that Mum and Dad were going to abandon the values of the Fellowship.

Unlike other members that we knew who were 'withdrawn from', we did not rush out to buy a television or a radio. Mum and Samantha did not throw their headscarves away. I still did not eat with the other children at school. In many ways nothing had changed.

Chapter Ten

After Being Shut Up

Suddenly, we found that we had acres of time to fill. The meetings had provided a rigid structure to our lives and now the time we had spent preparing for, travelling to and being at them was empty. Obviously, we had all lost our friends and family members who were still in the Fellowship, but I imagine it hit Mum and Dad the hardest. For Mum it must have seemed like a recurring nightmare first experienced in 1970, when she had bravely made the choice to stay with dad in the Fellowship, while the rest of her family had given up following the Fellowship leader, the 'Elect Vessel'.

He had taken over leading the Fellowship in the 1950s, and brought in most of the strict rules that forced us to live separately from the rest of the worldly people. I suppose Mum's family would have reluctantly stayed true to him as well, if he hadn't made a public spectacle of himself, fraternizing with women, swearing and drinking heavily at meetings and conferences.

Dad's family supported him, as did most of the local Fellowship, but Mum's parents had had enough of 'waiting

for the Lord to act'. For Mum it was a choice between family
and husband. Once she'd made the choice, that was it. She
even referred to her parents and brothers as the Open
Fellowship, which was the worst thing she could think of
saying about them. They were living a life that was as closed
off from the world as Mum and Dad, but saying that they
were Open was her way of calling them worldly.

The Lord did act in 1970, and the Elect Leader died, but
it was too late. The damage was done, and the family split.

I was just a child of seven when we were 'shut up', so they
kept their feelings from me. I sensed tension in the house,
and heard muffled voices behind closed doors that I pressed
my ear to. I wanted to know what was going on, but the
words that Mum and Dad kept reiterating were 'God is
punishing us for some reason.' The 'reason' was a mystery,
but I was growing up with Mum's mantra ringing in my
ears: 'Let the Lord into your heart and have faith.' The
punishment was exclusion from the Fellowship, the place
they still yearned to be. They questioned each other over and
over again: 'What have we done to deserve this?' Then they
comforted themselves with the fact that it was God's will.
With prayer, they believed, the answer would show itself to
them.

They were so wrapped up in their troubles that they
didn't worry too much about me after that, and I took advantage of this lack of supervision to further my friendships
with my worldly mates. I went to their houses, watched
television and played computer games.

One day after school I stopped off at my friend Leigh's
house. Leigh lived next door to a boy called Darrell. I went
with her hoping for a glimpse of the ginger-haired boy, on
whom I had developed a hopeless crush. But, despite my best

efforts to linger outside her house for as long as possible, I didn't see him.

I knew that in her kitchen there was a cupboard full of packets of crisps and I was hoping that she would offer me one. She didn't. Instead, her mum offered me a pear, which I took. I wish I hadn't. It wasn't ripe and I almost spat it out, but, not liking to be rude, I crunched my way through the whole damned thing. I was, however, appeased when we were offered the crisps, which we took upstairs with us. Her bedroom was very different from mine. Whereas mine was tidy and quite bare, except for a toy box and book shelves, hers was messy, with clothes all over the floor. She too had a dressing table, but hers was covered with makeup, music cassettes and a stereo player. On her walls were posters of the boy band Bros. I watched her as she kissed those twin brothers on the lips, declaring that she loved them. We were both rotund little girls, but, rather than wear skirts with elasticized-waistbands and baggy T-shirts as I did, she wore short denim skirts and jeans.

Leigh put a tape in the cassette player and she danced around the room, grabbing a lipstick on the way past her dressing table, which she daubed across her mouth while on the move. You may wonder if I was envious of this girl who seemed to have all the things I didn't. But I was not. I observed her and her posters, her music and her makeup, and I felt slightly repulsed by her. She looked so gaudy, and I couldn't think of anything worse than standing out like that. I actually felt a bit sorry for her.

My sister's worldly friend, Natalie, lived five houses down from us. Samantha hung around in the street with her, while I skirted around them on Samantha's old shopper bicycle. I knew that it would be passed on to me when

Samantha grew out of it, so I practised riding it. It was quite a move up from my little bike with stabilizers that Dad had picked up second-hand. Victor had spray-painted this bike red and blue for me.

I soon found that I could amuse Natalie better than Samantha could, and gradually Natalie spent more time with me than with my big sister. I could see that Samantha was distressed at this turn of events, but she didn't put up much of a fight. She did try to get her own back just once, though. The three of us were playing out and I was being my usual annoying self, butting in on their games, when Samantha suddenly called me.

'Lindsey, come over here, would you?' I felt wary. I could see a huge grin on my sister's face, which immediately told me something was up. It was common for Samantha to have a faraway, often worried, look on her face, but now she seemed alert and very much in the moment. With Natalie's persuasion, at last I sauntered over. I was certainly not going to hurry. Samantha grabbed my hand when I reached them and told me to open my mouth. No *way*, I thought to myself. I'm not *that* stupid. Then they said they had a chocolate for me. Well, that was quite another matter. I couldn't possibly pass up on this opportunity. Obediently, I opened my mouth, and waited for the treat.

'Yuk!' I spat on the ground with disgust. Far from the smooth, creamy chocolate I had expected, a Polo mint had been placed on my tongue. I hate sweets of any kind, apart from chocolate and fudge, so what might have been a nice surprise for most people was like a kick in the stomach for me. I'm not sure whether Natalie knew of my pet hate and had assumed that this was a nice surprise for me, or whether she was in on Samantha's despicable plans. Either way, it exposed a side of Samantha that I hadn't seen before. I was very impressed. She was more like me than I had thought!

I continued to build my friendship with Natalie, and we discovered that we got on really well. We must have looked an odd pair: I with my knee-length skirts and Hi-Tec trainers and she with her trendy jeans and Reeboks. We did have one thing in common, though, and that was our long hair. We both wore it tied back in a ponytail. The only difference was she did it out of choice, and I did it because I had to.

It didn't take me long to become a well-established part of Natalie's life. Every day after school I would rush to her house and knock for her to come out and play. She was two years older than I, so sometimes she had homework to do. So then I waited, hanging around in front of her house until she had finished.

I guess it was the natural course of things that I should go into her house. We played in the street. We played in her garden.

'Are you coming in, Lindsey?'

I didn't give too much thought to my reply. Not nearly as much as I probably should have done.

'Yep.'

And that was it. I was in. Surrounded by all the tempting things that I might have had access to before if Kerry's mum hadn't walked in on us or if I'd stayed friends with Leigh.

I got into the habit of going to Natalie's house every day after school. I knew that Mum wouldn't come until dinnertime to pick me up, so I had hours to kill and it wasn't long before I asked if I could watch the TV.

At first I couldn't really grasp what I was seeing. I couldn't distinguish between what was real and what wasn't. Anything with people in I thought was real life, but I did wonder how I was able to watch them. Did these people not know their lives were on telly. I felt much more at ease with the cartoons. At least I could see that they were drawings, even if they were moving. *ThunderCats* was my favourite.

One afternoon, I sat down in my usual position from where I could see Mum if she came up the garden path. I was looking forward to watching *ThunderCats* and *Alvin and the Chipmunks*, but Natalie had something else in mind.

'Let's watch a video,' she said. That sounded fine to me. I certainly wasn't going to let on I hadn't the faintest idea what a video might be.

'Which film do you want to see?' Natalie asked.

Oh dear! I thought.

My eyes darted between the two homemade videocassettes she held out to me. I had seen *Watership Down* and the musical *Annie* at Kerry's house, but that experience was not helping me in my decision. Natalie had seen lots of films, and I was afraid that, if I didn't take matters into my own hands, she would remember that what she really wanted to do was to go outside and play. If that happened my opportunity to watch television would be gone. I had to move quickly.

'Which do you want to see?' I enquired.

'I don't mind. I've already seen both.' She was beginning to sound bored already.

'Well,' I said, 'what's that one there?'

'*Pinocchio*,' she said, eyeing the cassette in her left hand. 'It's about a little boy whose nose grows bigger.'

It didn't sound particularly promising.

'What's the other one?' I asked hopefully.

'*Dirty Dancing.*'

I knew plenty about dancing – I loved my ballet books – but I couldn't begin to imagine why a dance would be dirty.

Whatever it was, it sounded more interesting than a little boy with a big nose.

'Let's watch that,' I said, trying not to let my excitement show.

Natalie put the cassette into the machine, undoubtedly wishing she were playing outside, or doing almost anything else at all.

Well, I'm glad I didn't choose to go outside and play, because I learned some things that day. As the video images stuttered into life I sat with my eyes glued to the television screen. I didn't want to miss one single moment.

'I'm not sure you should be doing this,' Natalie's mother said.

'It's fine,' I mumbled. In front of me, men and women gyrated, their bodies grinding against each other.

A women's voice was singing, 'And if I had the chance I'd never let you go.'

Natalie's mother left the room.

For the next two hours, I imagine that I am Baby, and that I am dancing in Johnny's arms. I am falling in love for the first time. And my lover is a fictional man called Johnny played by a film star. I am nine years old.

I found out later that the actor's name was Patrick Swayze, when Natalie bought me a full-length poster of him. I carried it home, rolled up tightly under my arm. It felt as if it were burning a hole in my side. Like a guilty criminal, I crept into the house, scurried upstairs and pushed that piece of filth under my bed, far out of sight. Every day for the next week I unrolled the paper and kissed the mouth of the man who looked back at me. I didn't care if his name was Patrick Swayze or Johnny Castle, the dance instructor he portrayed in the film. I was his Baby.

I couldn't stand the guilt for longer than a week. With one last kiss of regret, I screwed the poster into a ball and tossed it in a neighbour's dustbin.

I'm glad I watched *Dirty Dancing* that day. I felt that I had definitely made the right choice.

I may not have been able to stand the guilt of having the poster in my own house, but that did not stop me wanting to watch the film again. And again ... After I'd seen it for the third time, Natalie's patience snapped. 'For God's sake, Lin, let's go outside and play.' I was crushed by her bluntness, but I knew when to stop pushing my luck!

Instead, I relived the film over and over again in my head. In the privacy of my bedroom, concealed by my duvet, I held an imaginary man and kissed his lips. This was as close as I could expect to get to a member of the opposite sex for many years to come. I hoped to become a Fellowship girl again very soon, and if that happened I would meet my husband at the age of nineteen or twenty.

I continued to go to Natalie's house and became a regular fixture on their sofa in front of the TV. It really annoyed me when her dad and brother wanted to watch the motor racing. What a load of rubbish! I thought. It was noisy and as far as I could see no one was testing their own strength. It was cars doing all the work! I liked it better when *Roseanne* was on. Or *The Cosby Show*.

One Saturday afternoon Natalie's mum poked her head round the living room door.

'Do you want something to eat, Lindsey?' She understood that I was in no hurry to leave. In the back garden she was preparing a barbecue for friends. It was really time for me to go home, but I had never eaten a barbecue meal before, and I was always tempted by food.

'Yeah,' I said happily, 'I'll have something.'

'Lindsey,' Mum said when I arrived home. 'Dinner's on the table.'

I ate two dinners that night. My belly was fit to burst, but I didn't care. Patrick Swayze put his arms around me and I felt good.

I was becoming good at being two different people. At home I behaved like a Fellowship girl who listened to Dad reading the Bible and said my prayers at night. Outside the house I took part in the worldly things that my friends were doing without feeling guilty.

The Fellowship taught me always to expect that God would punish me for my sins, but it also taught me that anyone under the age of twelve was free of responsibility for their actions. As far as I was concerned, I could do pretty much anything and God would forgive me.

Natalie was older, but often looked to me for what we were going to do. When I was nine and she was eleven I thought it would be a good idea for us to start smoking. We picked half-smoked stubs off the ground, pocketed them and headed towards the school gates.

I did what I had done many times before, and scrambled over the top of the gates, dropping to the ground on the other side with a heavy thud. There was a gap underneath, but I had found out through bitter experience that, while Natalie could slide gracefully underneath, I couldn't.

We legged it up the school driveway and dashed around the corner, onto the field, and over to a thin row of bushes, carefully avoiding the school caretaker as we went. Once we were well hidden we began. It was more a case of inhaling a mouthful of acrid smoke and trying not to cough our guts up when it hit the back of our throats.

Following that initiation, we smoked on and off for a while, until even we couldn't overlook the fact that our regular supply of cigarettes came from dirty pavements, and filthy gutters. My habit didn't last long, and, after that, another nine years passed before I touched another cigarette.

Soon, Patrick Swayze wasn't the only man in my life. Everywhere I went I thought I saw the boy of my dreams. The boys of my dreams. At school, in the supermarket and in the museums I visited with Dad. It didn't matter that I didn't know them, and never would. I created their personalities in my head and thought I knew them. I watched my worldly friends practise kissing with the boys in the playground and, while they were crying over their breakups, I was kissing the back of my hand and hugging my pillow. I was trying to ensure that I would never be rejected; sometimes, though, I let my guard down.

The boy I had a crush on, Darrell, was a friend of Natalie's and lived just around the corner. One autumn evening, Natalie asked me if I wanted to go to a bonfire party Darrell was having at his house. Mum had warned me never, ever, to go out of the road, but I avoided being disobedient by entering his house through the back garden gate, which opened onto my street.

I watched fireworks shoot into the sky from beside a giant bonfire, which was steadily burning an effigy of Guy Fawkes. I couldn't count how many sins I was committing, but I knew that Satan must have been in my heart, because that night I went to bed dreaming about Darrell. The trouble was, I think he fancied Natalie, and resented the time I spent with her. I knew she was glad to have me to play with, as she definitely did not fancy him. But, despite this knowledge, I could not stop thinking about Darrell.

One day I was loitering in the street waiting for Natalie to come out and play, when he appeared in our street.

'All right?' He half nodded in my direction.

'Yeah, fine.' I felt myself blushing.

'Want a go on my skateboard?' he asked.

No, I most certainly did not, but I said yes, anyway. He handed me the board and I knelt down on it, trying hard not to let my bum show as my skirt rode up. I pushed off with my trailing leg and that was it: I was whizzing along. This felt good. What *have* I been worrying about? I asked myself, grinning. I couldn't help thinking, I bet Darrell thinks I look good.

Wham!

'*Aaaaahhh!*' I clutched my mouth, blood pouring down my chin. I had hit a crack in the pavement, catapulting me onto my face. Despite the pain, all I could think was, *Don't let Darrell see me, please.* I could see him sauntering over, casting a sly glance towards Natalie's house as he passed by. My pain disappeared into insignificance. Stupid, stupid, stupid! How *could* I have been so stupid? He wasn't interested in me. I learned a painful lesson that day. Worldly boys don't fancy girls like me. This fact was cemented a few weeks later when we passed in the street and he sneered at me, 'Your tits, they're just made of fat. They're not anything else.'

You might expect that at home I would be safe from hurtful comments, but I wasn't.

'Your head's too small for your body, Lindsey,' said Victor one day, and Samantha laughed. I looked in the mirror and wondered how my head could have shrunk. It looked the same size it had always been. Then I realized it was my body that was getting bigger.

But so what? I could still run round. I could still ride my bike and chase my friends up the street.

Anyway, it was common practice for us to take the mick out of each other. Not just in my family. Everyone in the Fellowship did it. It was as though anyone who was the least bit odd might pose a threat to the strength of our bond.

But then there were other comments.

'Of course you need more, Poppet,' Dad said one day when I asked Mum for another helping at dinner. 'You've got that big old belly to fill.' Did he *mean* that? I wasn't sure, but I knew he loved me, though. I was sure of that.

After school one day, I went into Mum's bedroom and flopped down on her mattress. I was looking forward to having a chat and telling her about my day. I watched her putting away the fresh washing, carefully pairing up socks and folding her knickers flat. It fascinated me that she wore two pairs of knickers. First she would put on a normal pair, as I and my sisters did, then cover these with what looked like an enormous band of elastic. I had no idea what these were supposed to do, but suspected that they had something to do with hiding her stomach. All I knew was she never went anywhere without them on.

I stretched out, flattening my own stomach with my hand, striking a glamour pose.

'I haven't got that much of a tummy, have I, Mum?' I asked hopefully.

Without taking her eyes off what she was doing, she replied briskly. 'That's just because the fat bit is hanging down onto the bed, Lindsey.'

That comment really hurt me, but I trusted Mum's judgement. If she thought I had a fat belly then I must have. She certainly wasn't going to boost my ego by telling me a lie. Actually, I rather suspect that she was just as critical of her own looks. To me she was perfect, but I had seen the way she scrutinized her image in her dressing table mirror. She inspected every inch of her face, picking at spots, trying to smooth out the blemishes. One tiny spot on her chin grew a regular supply of coarse black hairs. She used tweezers to pluck them out, but wouldn't wait for them to grow to a reasonable length before she attempted to remove the offending stubble. Often, this resulted in her gouging her face until the spot oozed clear liquid and eventually bled. I hated seeing her do this and usually took the implement from her hand, and went about the task myself, applying a lot more care.

Mum had grown up with the restricted dress code that I was now at the mercy of. Instead of celebrating her body, and mine, she saw it as something to hide and be ashamed of. She did not have any qualms about making sure I followed her example.

'This would look nice on you,' Mum said to me one morning. She was leafing through a catalogue that had been pushed through our front door. It was full of gadgets and trinkets, featured because they looked really useful in the catalogue, but never actually came in handy for anything. I went over to look at what she was pointing to, excited that I might be getting something new. It wasn't even my birthday. My heart sank when I saw the picture. Posing, with a bright smile on her face, was a middle-aged lady wearing a grey skirt with an elasticized waist, made of some kind of hard-wearing material. Mum must have seen my disappointment because she said kindly, 'It comes in green as well.'

I came to accept that my clothes, as well as having to comply with Fellowship rules, would be limited in choice because of my expanding waistline. By the time I was ten years old, the skirts that most of my worldly friends were wearing were becoming noticeably shorter. I felt pretty peeved by this. My time of not standing out was coming to an end.

What I could have done to keep up with my trendy friends was wear fashionable shoes. Shoes were the one item of women's clothing the Fellowship did not have a strong opinion about.

Unfortunately, I was still wearing my T-bar clodhoppers, which was really embarrassing. This was because my feet were extra wide and these were the only ones I could find that fitted! For the other Fellowship girls, their shoes offered them a rare opportunity to show off. If one girl turned up with some fantastic footwear, within days the rest would have the same thing. It was very competitive. I loved shoes and at one time I had twenty pairs of them.

Mum was determined that her money spent on the hideous T-bars would not be wasted, and wasn't concerned about my vanity. But I had other ideas. I would not be wearing the horrible T-bars at school. Instead I put a pair of trainers in my rucksack, and when I arrived I found a quiet spot in the playground and did a quick swap. The trainers were Hi-Tec, so it meant that I still wouldn't be *that* trendy, but it made the best of a bad job.

At school my appearance did not go unnoticed. During the lunch break the kids would sometimes play kiss chase. 'Lindsey, come and play,' my girlfriends would shout to me.

'We don't want her,' was the general attitude of the boys. On one memorable occasion, I was saved from the embarrassment of having to excuse myself from the game by a girl shouting, 'Lindsey doesn't play – it's against her religion.'

This time I was glad that someone else had opened her mouth and let out a thoughtless comment. It shielded me from having to go through the torturous process of the boys singling me out as the one they didn't want to kiss. I would much rather be seen as religious than so unattractive that no one wanted to touch me.

One of the boys, Alex, was particularly cruel. We had got off on the wrong foot when we started school. One afternoon we were sitting in the classroom, and I was watching him swing back and forth on his chair. I was half hoping the seat would slip out from underneath him because I hated him. He thought he was the hardest boy in the school, and really cool. I couldn't stand that kind of obvious brawn. In his hand he was flexing a plastic ruler, the kind that is not meant to shatter. He said out loud to no one in particular. 'I bet I can break this.' His attempts to do so were futile and, without thinking, I reached over and snatched the ruler from his hands. 'Let me have a go,' I said, and snapped it. He was furious. 'You stupid cow,' he yelled. Inside I cringed. I hated being at the receiving end of anyone's anger, and always did my best not to upset people. I felt surprised that I had almost deliberately gone looking for trouble. If I was going to succeed in not standing out, I would have to watch myself a bit more carefully in future.

Chapter Eleven

The Move

I was finding my feet in the world, despite its chal-
lenges, and managing to put hopes of rejoining the
Fellowship to the back of my mind. I had worked out how
to fill my spare time and, on the whole, I was left to my own
devices. My only reminder of Fellowship ritual was at
dinnertime, when Dad read lengthy passages from the Bible.
I watched with despair as my plate of food got colder and
colder, while, at the same time, trying to stay reverent of
the fact that Dad was preaching from the most important
book in our house. I discreetly held my hands over the plate
in a feeble attempt to hold in the rapidly escaping heat. Just
when I thought he was wrapping up the long list of who
begot whom, he'd pick up his hymnbook. I'd groan inwardly,
wondering where God was when I needed him. If it was my
lucky day, we'd sing only one or two hymns, then we'd close
our eyes to say thanks. I squeezed my eyelids together, fear-
ing that, if I didn't, God might think I wasn't taking it seriously and put the idea in Dad's head that I needed to hear
some more verses of scripture to make me into a better
Christian.

The words 'Thank you for this food before us, in the name of the Lord Jesus Christ, amen' were like music to my ears. At last, I was allowed to tuck in, and I shovelled the lukewarm food into my mouth gratefully.

I may have been filling my time successfully, but Dad obviously was not. He suddenly decided it would be a good idea to occupy our Sunday afternoons by going on long walks in the countryside. I hated these walks with a passion, as they took me away from my playing, or, rather, Natalie's TV.

Dad always strode off ahead, his long legs eating up the miles and making nothing of the gates and stiles we encountered. He carried a map in a waterproof holder around his neck, and clutched a compass in his hand. We were only strolling a few miles in the Home Counties, for God's sake, not the bloody Pyrenees. Mum hobbled behind on her arthritic ankles, her face wincing with pain, and I stayed at her side, chattering nonstop. When Dad had completely disappeared out of view I'd start to worry. I couldn't carry Mum on my own if her ankles gave out, and Samantha was often out of earshot, ambling along on her own, a grin on her face, plucking flowers from the hedgerows, somewhere between us and Dad.

'Dad,' I'd roar. 'Wait for us.' But my calls usually went unheeded. Eventually, Mum and I would find Dad, leaning casually against a stone wall.

'Where have you been?' he'd shout cheerfully. And Mum and I would grimace at each other.

If I was lucky, there would be a shop along the route and we'd buy ice creams. Having polished mine off, I'd grill Mum about what we were going to have for dinner when we got home. If it was something I liked, I felt spurred on, perhaps even catching up with Dad, and feeling guiltily irritated with Mum for taking so long. If the menu wasn't so good, I'd wear Mum down with repeated suggestions for what I could have instead, or at least what I could have it with. By the time we got home I was more than ready for my dinner.

It seemed that life without the Fellowship wasn't as bad as I'd feared it might be.

Then my parents made an announcement that would change my life.

They told Samantha and me that we were going to sell our house in Albion Avenue and move to one that was detached. It was their last desperate attempt to demonstrate to God their commitment to the Fellowship and its values. The Fellowship had made it clear several years previously that members' homes should not be joined to worldly homes. The rule went as far as to say that driveways shouldn't be shared, and access to Fellowship houses' drainage systems should be on Fellowship property. This was their interpretation of 'being in the world but not part of the world'. The rule had been invented long after many Fellowship members had bought houses that did not fit this criterion, so there was a period of leniency, while members gathered together the funds, and energy, in preparation for the move to a detached house.

I knew that this was seriously bad news for me and I felt frightened. Realizing that my worldly friends would be unlikely to be allowed to visit me in our new home, I took a dim view of my future.

The process of selling our house and moving was a long one. The difficulty was finding a house that would be approved by the Fellowship, if they ever cared to visit us again. Eventually, the right one, at the right price, was located. It was worse than I had even dared to fear. We were to move to another town. It was only eight miles down the road, but it might as well have been a thousand. I had to leave my worldly friends and that was that.

Moving day came and I stood with Natalie as Mum and Dad travelled back and forth between the house and the removal van, lugging crates packed with every item that we owned. At last we were ready to go. In the fading daylight I said goodbye to Natalie, my dear friend who had no idea how much she had done to help me stay sane during the last few years.

It was 1991, I was eleven years old, and I had never felt more alone in my life.

Chapter Twelve

Secondary Education

We moved in December, during the school Christmas holidays, but this was not a problem for my parents. For us, the season wasn't one of celebration, thanks to yet another Fellowship rule. The Ministry might have been better off publishing just one sentence on one page, saying, 'Fun, of any kind, forbidden,' rather than the many volumes that members were required to slog through.

On Christmas Day we would very often drive out to Beachy Head, the windiest spot on the south coast. While everyone else in the world tucked into roast turkey, roast potatoes and Christmas pudding, we would walk, often in pouring rain, feeling the gusts of wind snatching at our hair. To make matters worse, Mum always cooked a turkey at some point during the holiday, really rubbing in the fact that we would have turkey if we wanted, but not as a celebration of Jesus's birth. I didn't care, anyway. I didn't even like turkey that much.

I had, however, been introduced to Christmas elsewhere and usually managed to enjoy myself in spite of the lack of festivities at home. I first encountered Christmas celebrations at primary school. One winter's day I came into school to find my classroom had been transformed. It was sparkling, red gold and silver. A tree stood in the corner, dripping with tinsel, baubles and little lights.

My jaw dropped. I had never seen anything so beautiful. What astonished me even more was one of the walls. It appeared to me to be covered in silver foil and, as far as I knew, the only place that silver foil came from was the wrapper of a Kit Kat. I stood looking at the shiny wall feeling massive admiration for my teacher, Ms De Palmer, who, I thought, had managed to consume enough of these delicious treats to collect the foil that now covered her classroom wall.

Over the years I helped Natalie decorate the tree at her house. I stood side by side with Natalie and her mother, hanging up the baubles and tinsel with great reverence. The meaning of the celebration was lost on me, but I relished the feeling of closeness it gave me with that family. Natalie's Mum had a red dress that clung to her curves, which she wore at Christmas time. I thought she looked beautiful and vowed that one day I would have a dress just like it. Without Natalie living around the corner, I knew Christmas would be different for me from then on.

A few months before we moved I started at the same secondary school as Natalie. I hadn't felt the same joy at attending this school as I had when I started primary. By this time I was wary of worldly children, and dreaded the prospect of having to meet a new load of kids who might find me weird. In particular, I feared the religious education lessons that were on the timetable.

On the morning of my first RE lesson, Mum sent me to school with a note that excused me from attending it. This was common practice for Fellowship children. The Fellowship thought that other religions were evil and that we should not expose ourselves to their teachings. When the time came, I entered the classroom with every other child in my tutor group, but, instead of finding myself a chair as they did, I stood next to the desk at the front of the room.

The RE teacher was a small man, who bounced around excitedly. I immediately took a dislike to him. His face was smooth, clean-shaven, and made him look deceptively young. He wore a sharp suit, and his shirt collar was fastened with a shiny tie. 'Sit down, sit down,' he called to the class, smiling animatedly. I didn't move from where I was, and, when he became aware of me still standing beside him, the smile vanished from his face.

'What is it?' he barked at me.

I silently handed over the note that I had been holding in my hand. He ripped open the envelope and cast his eyes over the paper. Without looking at me he instructed me to sit at the back of the classroom. I felt overcome by fear, and confused. Wasn't he going to let me go to the library? I had heard that this was what other Fellowship children did during RE lessons. I couldn't stay in the classroom while he talked about evil ideas. 'Can't I go to the library?' I asked timidly. 'Nope, there's no one to look after you, you'll have to stay here.' He looked at me when he said this. Was it my imagination, or was he almost relishing being able to disrespect my religious beliefs? He certainly looked it. I didn't have it in me to challenge him any further, so, with cheeks hot with embarrassment, I stumbled to the back of the room and sat down.

Even worse was to come. A few weeks into the term, he announced that the class would be going on a trip to visit a church. I usually sat trying not to listen to the ungodly words that were spoken during the lesson, but this time my ears caught what he was saying. I felt my palms go sweaty; what was I to do now? I knew that attending the trip was out of the question, as the only place of worship I was allowed to enter was a Fellowship meeting room, and I hadn't even been inside one of *them* for four years.

Details of the trip were given out to all of us and I left the classroom with a heavy heart. That night, I broached the subject with Mum. What I really wanted was for her to say, 'Oh, don't worry about that, Lindsey, you can stay at home that day.' But, of course, nothing was ever that easy. 'You'll have to stay at school,' was all she said. I knew it was unlikely that I could do that, as I wasn't even allowed to leave the classroom when the class were there, let alone when they wouldn't be. 'Can't you just write me a note saying I've got a dentist appointment?' I begged. She was dismissive of this idea as it was a downright lie. Mum and Dad never lied. If they had been prepared to do so, we might never have been 'withdrawn from'. I should have known they wouldn't start just for the sake of an RE trip.

I decided to take matters into my own hands and wrote a note myself, excusing me from the trip, and asked Natalie to fake my mum's signature. She did, but, looking over it, I could see that the efforts of an eleven-year-old and a thirteen-year-old were not going cut it. I screwed up the letter and tried to think of something else.

I ran through the possibilities in my head. One option was skiving off school, but I had never done this and felt even more scared of wandering around town on my own than I did of getting caught. And I would inevitably be caught as I couldn't even go to the places that most kids hung out when playing truant, such as the amusement arcade or a café. In the end I decided I would just have to face it out.

When I told my teacher that Mum didn't want me to go on the church trip, his loathing for me was clear. 'You have to. You can't stay here,' he stated. This time I had to challenge him, so I said, 'Perhaps I can join another class, or something.' I certainly didn't want to do this either. This would mean that my religious differences would spill beyond the wall of this classroom into another. This thought was almost unbearable, but I knew I had to bear it. I would recover from this excruciating embarrassment, but I might not recover from the evil I would encounter in the church.

Tiring of me, he said, 'Go and see Mrs Bates, she can sort it out.' Mrs Bates was our head of year and had been only a distant figure in assemblies up until this point. I now went to assemblies, as at secondary school they were nonreligious, and simply a convenient time for everyone to gather in one place and receive important notices from the teachers. There certainly weren't any hymns or prayers to fret about. That was one advantage of secondary school and, as far as I could see, the only one. On trembling legs I walked down the quiet corridor. Everyone was in their lessons, and I felt conspicuous as I passed classroom doors with windows, through which children peered at me as I made my way to the office.

When I reached Mrs Bates's room I looked at the closed door for a few moments, my heart pounding, before I knocked. 'Come in,' she called. I opened the door into what seemed like an enormously long room. I stood in the doorway, until she ushered me in with a call. The walk to her desk, at the far end of the room, seemed to take years to complete.

At last I was standing in front of her. She didn't get up, but carried on writing, her pen moving carefully over the paper that lay before her. At last she looked up, and without any pleasantries got straight to the point. 'I understand that you are refusing to go on the trip to the church,' she said. I felt taken aback. So she already knew who I was.

The realization that I had been discussed in the school staffroom, and everyone knew that I was a child with religious differences that made her life difficult, suddenly dawned on me. All my attempts to blend in and be anonymous had failed dismally. But, instead of feeling angry at the people whose religious beliefs had put me in this awful situation, I felt defensive of them. With my lower lip being forced down at the corners by my uncontrollable desire to cry, I did my best to defend the religion I had been taught to love and respect.

Chapter Thirteen

Coming of Age

The move meant that I had to change schools after one term.

A place became available at a secondary school which was only a mile away from my new house. Of the three schools I could have been sent to, it was my preferred choice, but even that didn't make me feel any less terrified about going. I'd always hated returning to school after lunch when all the other kids had formed their groups, and now I was arriving a whole term after everyone else. I imagined that all eyes would be on me, the new girl, and standing out was the last thing I wanted to do.

I needn't have worried because my new classmates, after a fleeting moment of interest when I was brought into their French lesson and introduced to them, seemed far more preoccupied with chatting and throwing screwed up balls of paper at the bespectacled male French teacher. Dodging the missiles, he looked around with a bemused expression on his face, asking vaguely, 'Does anyone want to look after … what's your name?'

A couple of girls put their hands up and he waved me in the general direction of one of them sitting in the front row of desks. I took this to mean I should join her, so I scuttled over to sit in the vacant chair at her desk. She introduced herself as Nicola.

Something about her reminded me of a girl I'd met at my last school who had picked on me.

One afternoon she grabbed my pencil case, and started taking everything out of it. I felt outraged, but said nothing. She held up a pen that had been given to me as a gift from Mum. She knew this one was special to me, but demanded that I should lend it to her. Helplessly I looked on as she proceeded to use it throughout the rest of the lesson. I reassured myself that she would give it back when the class was over. She did not.

Having packed it into her pencil case with her pens and pencils, she got up and started pulling on her coat. I didn't know what to say, but managed to stutter, 'Er, Nicola, can I have my pen back … please?' She smiled serenely and told me she'd bring it to school the next day. I hadn't come across this kind of behaviour before, and had no idea how to manage the situation.

The next day at school things had taken a turn for the worse with regard to the pen incident. Just as I sat down, another girl in my class called Emily walked by our desk. She smiled sweetly at me, and I smiled back feeling uneasy.

It was then I noticed the pen in her hand. It was mine. I looked at Nicola. She had a half smile across her face. I looked back at Emily, and she stared back, a challenging look in her eye. 'Thanks for letting me use your pen, Nicola,' she said to the now grinning girl next to me. I didn't get the pen back, and I decided to move to another desk after that.

* * *

The day I started at my new secondary was marked by another landmark event in my life. I rushed home from school, so glad to have survived the first day, and dashed upstairs to change out of my school uniform. Mum was standing in the hall when I came pounding back down to grab an apple and packet of crisps before intending to go back up to my room to read my book.

As I leapt down the steps my green elasticized skirt flew up, revealing my knickers. When I reached the bottom, Mum said, 'Lindsey, open your legs.' I stood there aghast. Whatever did she mean? Obediently, I spread my legs apart and Mum crouched and peered up my skirt, hooking it up with her hand. I was worried. What had she seen?

For as long as I could remember I had been terrified that a snake or slug might enter my body through my private hole down there. This terrifying thought had developed after I'd read a book about refugee children from London who went to live in the countryside to escape the bombs of the Blitz. One of the stories vividly described the plight of a little girl who had the misfortune to be placed with a woman who thought it enough to put a roof over her head, and didn't extend her hospitality to food and baths.

I read with interest about this poor girl, who was obviously so much in need of love, and felt sorry for her. The part that really filled me with horror described how she went to the toilet one evening and, on pulling down her pants and proceeding with her business, discovered a long white worm coming out of her bumhole. She said she pulled and pulled at it and eventually it released itself from her body with a pop. This image had lingered in my mind for a long time after, and it came back to me as Mum gazed at my privates.

'You've got your period,' she said matter-of-factly.

The relief was massive. There was no snake or worm, but rather blood. 'Oh, right,' I said cheerfully. 'What do I do now?'

'I'll get you a pad,' said Mum, and we both went upstairs to sort out my predicament. An hour later I came downstairs again feeling worried. Mum was in the kitchen chopping vegetables for dinner. 'Er, Mum,' I said doubtfully, 'I'm still bleeding.'

My knowledge about such matters was extremely limited, and hadn't been helped much by the literature Mum had discreetly placed on my pillow when I was seven years old. I had picked up the flimsy reading material wondering what storybook Mum had picked up from the charity shop this time.

The cover hadn't given much away, and on opening the leaflet I had a shock. On the first page was a sketchy drawing of a naked girl, and, inset, a detailed diagram of her vagina. I had looked at the drawings without much interest. I had seen my own naked body many times and saw nothing new here. I didn't even bother to try to understand the picture of the vagina. It looked like a pretty messy thing and I wasn't keen to find out any more about it.

On turning over the page, however, I was delighted to see a drawing of something I hadn't seen for a long time. A picture of a naked boy, and, more importantly, a willy. I gazed at the crude drawing for several minutes, trying to work out what a boy did with it. Didn't it get caught in his pants?

The book gave me some helpful information. 'Don't worry,' it said, 'if while on the bus home from school you get an erection.' An 'erection' I had discovered, was when a boy's willy gets hard. It seemed to me that a willy was a bit of a liability. I turned to the second book. This was a bit more like it! This one had photographs of real live willies. Now I knew what every other worldly girl knew, I thought. I couldn't be thought of as naïve about boys now I was armed with all this crucial knowledge.

I think I must have missed the part about the menstrual cycle, but now, in the kitchen with Mum, I vaguely recalled skipping over some pictures of some horrific-looking contraptions that a girl was supposed to wear, and things to put inside her when she had her period. I hadn't taken in the part about how long the bleeding would last, though. Now Mum imparted this vital information. 'Oh, you'll bleed for about a week,' she said.

'A week?' I was aghast.

'You might have some pain, too. I used to be in agony,' she added, 'until I had children. Then the pain eased a bit.'

Oh, great! I thought; it just gets better and better.

About this time we had a visit from a family member who had something else to tell us about children. When I was growing up, all I knew about Mum's family was that she had a mother and father and two brothers, but had nothing to do with them. They lived in Croydon, the opposite side of London, so there was little chance of bumping into them, but that was not why we didn't see them. I was told that they were worse than worldly people, as they had had the chance to join our branch of the Fellowship, but chose not to. They decided to follow another slightly more liberal-minded leader.

I do recall pictures of Mum's parents in the house, tucked away in a drawer of the piano stool. Occasionally, Mum would talk about them and mention her youngest brother, Roderick, and her other brother, Trevor, in passing. When

Mum recounted memories of her family, she seemed happy and her face relaxed. I didn't give them much thought, really, and it never occurred to me that one day I'd a have the chance to meet them.

The only time I came close was when I was eleven years old. Mum was a bit of a curtain twitcher, always checking what was going on outside. On this occasion, she was peering out of the bay window from where she could see the street, when she called to my dad, 'I think that's Mum. My mum's just gone past in a car.'

We all rushed to the window. I was so excited. Never having met Mum's family, I had no idea what they might look like since all the pictures we had were over twenty years old. Inside the car was my Uncle Roderick and his family, but they looked nothing more than shadows from where I was standing.

The car came back down the street and stopped outside. Uncle Roderick got out and began walking to the door. Mum went to see him but their conversation didn't last more than a few minutes. I couldn't hear what was said because Dad was keeping us at a safe distance, behind the closed door of the living room. But what we learned from it was that Uncle Roderick had two children, Alec and Chloe, and my Uncle Trevor also had two, Amelia and Keith. In return, Mum told him about my birth. She had never told them and expected this to be news, but somehow they had already found out. I'd been alive for eleven years, so I suppose it wasn't surprising that the news had got back to them.

Mum was a real gossip hound, so the temptation to chat and find out what was happening in their lives must have been irresistible. Still, she came to her senses, and, like the abiding Fellowship follower that she was, Mum eventually sent him away, without inviting him in. Maybe Roderick's family had heard that we were 'withdrawn from', and were hoping for a reunion. They must have been disappointed.

The surprise visit aroused a curiosity in me. Suddenly, the people who had been little more than faceless names, seemed real, with lives and families of their own. At school my classmates often spoke about their own families. At these times I stayed quiet and tried to look as though I were really busy reading from my textbooks. What could I say about mine? All the kids knew that I was religious, my removal from religious-education lessons having made sure of this. However, I felt unable to share with them what was really going on.

If asked, I mentioned my nephews and niece, Alice's children, whom I had never met, but had knowledge of from Mum, who took it upon herself to rifle through my sister's medical records that were filed at the hospital where she worked. I would be vague, not liking to lie, and say my family were fine, but I didn't see them very often. It didn't occur to me that kids at school might have a completely accepting attitude towards my strange life. I felt so strange myself that it seemed impossible to think that they could.

I invited none of these classmates to my house, so no one saw that the only people in my life were my parents and my sister. There was a girl called Stephanie in my tutor group, and I found out that she lived around the corner from me. We took to walking to and from school together.

She would turn up at my house in the morning and knock for me. I never invited her in and she accepted without question the rules that I imposed on her. My flourishing friendship with Stephanie wasn't without its problems, though. Having started at the school a term before I had, the others were already settled into their friendship groups. Stephanie had become friendly with two girls, Kimberly and Eve. In particular, Kimberly was very possessive over her relationship with Stephanie, and saw my arrival as a threat. At first I was unaware that I was causing a rift in the group of three girls, but Kimberly and Eve soon saw to it that I knew.

One morning I entered the wooden annexe that was our temporary maths classroom, and after scouring the room I spotted Stephanie sitting at the back. Eve was on the chair next to her, but the desk in front of them was vacant. I made my way to it and plonked my bag down on the table. I smiled at the girls and sat down. Immediately, Eve leaned forward and said, 'You can sit with Kimberly if you like.' She pointed helpfully to where Kimberly was sitting, some distance away. I thought to myself, No, thanks. But to her I said 'No, that's really kind, but I'll sit here, thanks.'

'No, really, you can,' she persisted. I noticed that Stephanie's smile was a bit strained, but couldn't think why. I turned round and got on with my work. Halfway through the lesson it hit me. Why hadn't I realized it before? What Eve was saying was, 'I don't want you sitting near me and Stephanie, so just move.' As soon as this realization hit me I wanted the floor to swallow me up. I felt so stupid. I had let Eve make a fool of me.

I had always been so careful to try not to let people see my weaknesses, and now I had shown Eve mine, by not cottoning on to the fact she was being manipulative with her comments. I felt so angry with myself. It was everything to me to stay one step ahead of people so that I could protect myself from their malice and spite.

One particular morning I arrived at school earlier than everyone else. Stephanie was ill, so hadn't come to pick me up, and I got a lift from Mum, who was on her way to work in the car. I was the first one there, so I took the prime position on top of the heater at the back of the classroom.

It was the middle of winter and freezing cold in the annexe that was my form room. I huddled there, my legs swinging against the metal grille that covered the wall-mounted radiator. The only part of me that seemed to be heating up was my bum, which was rapidly becoming unbearably hot as warm air blasted through my thin skirt. I shivered inside my duffle coat, wishing that Stephanie was there to keep me company. I felt vulnerable on my own, as I knew the boys would start arriving soon.

Usually, they kept themselves to themselves, choosing to scrap with each other rather than interact with girls. Sometimes, though, they tired of their inane behaviour and, having not yet developed the true art of flirting, began shouting abuse at a chosen female instead. I certainly didn't attract that kind of 'positive' attention! I feared that they might comment instead on my lack of attractiveness, which would be even worse.

It wasn't boys who arrived next, though, but someone I welcomed even less: Kimberly. I groaned inwardly but, as she entered, I smiled pleasantly at her and said hi.

'God, you look like a sumo wrestler sitting there,' she said without so much as a hello to get warmed up. That wiped the smile off my face.

Chapter Fourteen

Feeling the Strain

Since our move, Samantha had started college, doing Pitman training. She had the ideal hands for typing: long slim fingers that were double-jointed. She had always made me and Victor squeal with disbelief and horror at her ability to bend her fingers back without any discomfort. Many times I had sat and watched them skim over piano keys at the speed of lightning, without any regard for timing or hitting the correct notes. Now she was putting them to good use, preparing to hit the world of work.

I was so wrapped up in my life at school and trying to maintain a low profile that I hadn't taken much notice of Samantha since we moved house. We each had our own rooms, and I didn't think much about the amount of time she spent in there. If I'm honest, I found interacting with her awkward, and tried to brush her off with a smile. A quick 'Hello', and I'd dash into the privacy of my room. It wasn't until I was forced to share a bedroom with her again that I became fully aware of how much distance had come between us.

I was twelve years old when Victor came back into our lives declaring he needed a break and Mum's home cooking.

Mum welcomed him with open arms, and told him he could have my bedroom.

He told us nothing about his life or the women he'd been seeing, but arrived with a ladies' cardigan and lipstick amongst his things. Not wanting anything to go to waste, Mum tried the cardigan on to see if it fitted, and threw it in the dustbin when it didn't. She tipped the lipsticks in the bin but kept the little cosmetic bag they came in. I was far more interested to find out where he had been and what he had been up to.

I noticed that he'd brought a little black address book home with him, so I decided I would take a peek inside as soon as I got the chance.

At the first opportunity, I rummaged through his, or rather my, bedside cabinet. I quickly located what I was after. I leafed through it, not sure what I was hoping to find. I scanned the lists of telephone numbers, noting that many were accompanied by the names of women. I felt a streak of jealously flit through my body. He was my brother, and here was a list of faceless names who had shared a part of his life that I knew nothing about. I chose the name at random, something like Anita, and dialled the telephone number next to it. Before anyone could answer I put the phone down, horrified at what I was doing.

Sharing a room with Samantha once more gave us the chance to get reacquainted. She talked endlessly about the boys she had met at college, and how she wished she could have a boyfriend. She was seventeen years old and yearning to do what all good Fellowship girls did: find a mate and settle down. My heart ached for her. She read her Bible every day, several times a day, and questioned Mum over and over again about when we would go back to the Fellowship. Mum gave her standard answer about God knowing best, but I knew that even she was tiring of the wait.

Samantha's reading matter, apart from the Bible and Ministry books, consisted of magazines about the royal family. She would pore over photographs of Princess Diana, Sarah Ferguson and the Queen. She fell in love with Princess Anne's son and I teased her about her crush mercilessly.

At her request, my parents, Samantha and I travelled down to London for the Trooping of the Colour. As we stood among the cheering crowds I felt the familiar sense of embarrassment flood through me. No one else had a head-scarf on and most women were dressed in jeans or shorts. I was aware of the television cameras behind us, mounted on the Victoria memorial, awaiting the arrival of the Queen onto the balcony of Buckingham Palace, and began to wonder if we should be there. I remembered that a leader of the Fellowship had condemned members for lining the streets with worldly people to watch the marriage of Prince Charles to Diana. He must have really had something against them, as he predicted in 1981 that the marriage wouldn't last.

Another time we went to the Ebbw Vale Garden Festival in Wales. It was a bit like a big party, but Samantha was not in a partying mood. I think Mum and Dad regretted the outing pretty soon after we started out in the car. It was a four hours drive to Wales, Samantha was not behaving well and wasn't thinking twice about trying to hit Dad, who was driving. I cringed into my seat, and closed my eyes.

We had a terrible day, and travelled home in the dark, in silence. Samantha sat in the back of the car with me, picking at the skin on her hands. I squinted at my magazine, which was lit intermittently by the orange motorway lights that we passed. The magazine had film and television reviews in it, and I stared at the photo of a scene from one of the films. Suddenly I put the magazine up against the car window. I pressed my face to the photo and stared into it. I willed it to come alive like a television screen. I wanted to escape from this madness so much.

Chapter Fifteen

Reading Matters

Every day Victor drove off to work in his big white van. It was always touch and go whether he would get the thing to start. He'd turn the key in the ignition several times, pulling out the choke as far as it would go, and eventually it would splutter into life. He was working as a carpenter and had his own business, and I felt proud of him. He had followed the path of a typical Fellowship man, and I saw this as a positive sign that, if the chance came to go back to the Fellowship, he would come with us. I could hardly bear to think that he might not.

Knowing that he would be out all day, and inspired by my finding of the little black book, I resumed my nosing in Victor's temporary bedroom. After school one day, I came home and the house was empty. I had taken to going into his bedroom and trying on his jeans. I had never worn trousers before, so the feeling of my legs being enclosed by material was strange.

His normal jeans were straight-legged and didn't fit my plump thighs that well, so, on this occasion, I was pleased to see that he had left his work jeans on the bedroom floor.

These were baggier in the leg. I put them on, adding a pair of high-heeled platforms, to make me look a bit more feminine. I threw on one of Victor's large T-shirts as well and tottered downstairs to flounce around in front of the long mirror that was attached the wall in the hallway. Next, I strutted through the house, all the while having animated conversations with my latest imaginary boyfriend.

I based all my imaginary boyfriends on real boys. I fancied every single boy in my class at school at some point during my five years there, possibly every boy in the entire school. In bed at night, I snuggled under my covers and began my fantasy life. I imagined the preferred boy of the moment scaling the wall outside my window and climbing in to join me. I made the fantasy as real as possible by working out every detail: how he'd get up the wall (he'd climb onto the porch, which had a flat roof and was directly below my bedroom window), and how he'd get in (I had a large wooden-framed window that swung open wide enough to accommodate a small boy). I never felt bad at night while I was in my own little world, but in the morning I could barely look anyone in the face. I fantasized so hard about these boys, and in so much detail, that I when I got to school I almost believed that one would come over and hold my hand as if he actually were my boyfriend.

I started blushing violently and this didn't go unnoticed. At the table, one dinnertime, Victor asked me to pass him the salt and I immediately felt my cheeks redden. I couldn't bear this public display of embarrassment, and bent right over my chair, as if reaching for something on the floor.

'What are you doing, Lindsey?' Victor asked when I hadn't surfaced after a few moments.

'I've lost my fork,' I mumbled. By now I was wishing I hadn't dropped my head so far down, as, instead of the blood leaving my cheeks, it was staying put. When it became impossible for me to stay bent down any longer, I pulled myself back up, beads of sweat starting to form on my forehead. Victor looked at me, a slight grin on his face. 'You're blushing,' he commented.

I was having another good old rummage around in Victor's room when I found a soft-porn novel under the bed. It was a paperback with a blue cover and gold lettering. It looked well thumbed and at first I assumed it was another one of Mum's pickings from the charity shop.

Without a TV or a social life, I whiled away long hours reading and rereading my favourite books. I loved the Famous Five books and *Swallows and Amazons*, anything about perfect children in perfect worlds. When I was really little, Mum would look at books with me, sitting by my head, stroking my cheek, and she'd still be reading aloud as I fell asleep. I joined the local library when I was old enough. For some reason this wasn't banned in our household, but this could have been because Mum and Dad loved reading as much as I did. Mum would choose her Miss Read and Brother Cadfael whodunit mystery books, while I raced off to the children's section.

My feet would clatter loudly on the highly polished parquet floor, and echo around the high-ceilinged building. I loved the feeling of calm that came over me when I stepped off the busy street, roaring with cars, into the cool building. It was deathly quiet in there and the few people who browsed the shelves spoke in whispers to each other. Beyond the main library was the reading room, where I saw old men falling asleep over their newspapers.

The walls in the children's section seemed to me to be sky-high with shelves, every one jam-packed with books. When I first started coming I had studied the shelving system carefully and now knew exactly where every genre of book was located. It didn't take me long to read through all the younger children's books and, by the age of eight, I was moving on to moderately thick paperbacks about ponies and ballet dancers. I wanted to ride horses and I wanted to be a ballet dancer, but I wasn't allowed lessons in either activity. I rode my first pony in the living room of our first house. He was the piano stool and I held string reins as I spurred him on. I danced my first dance there, too, humming music to myself as I clumsily spun around the room.

The book I was now holding in my hands in Victor's room looked nothing like any of the books I had seen before. I sat down on the bed and turned over the cover to the first page. It was basically about a load of people who worked on a porn magazine. As far as I can remember, the plot was pretty thin, but it wasn't the plot I was interested in. On just about every page there were explicit descriptions of people having sex, in every imaginable position. For the first time in my life I was introduced to the idea of two people of the same sex getting it on together. The idea of two blokes having sex really turned me on, and I felt my body responding.

Quite honestly, that novel taught me everything I might ever need to know about sex, and about the porn industry. Having skimmed through the entire book, deliberately targeting the pages with the raunchiest scenes on them, I put it back under Victor's bed. Something had been awoken in me, and there was no going back.

After my encounter with that book it wasn't the *children's* section of the library that I headed for. I discovered Jackie Collins, Shaun Hutson and various other authors who shared with me their knowledge of all things sexual. I now judged books by how much sex was in them, and how explicit they were. The more the better as far as I was concerned.

The books guided me to my own pleasurable parts, and I soon became obsessed with masturbating. I did it at every opportunity, sometimes hiding in the toilet, while Samantha banged on the door to get in. No one had ever talked to me about any of this stuff, and certainly not my own parents. All I had ever seen was Mum push Dad off as he tried to kiss her. But somehow, despite this, I didn't feel guilty about what I was doing. I thought that, if God hadn't meant us to enjoy ourselves, he wouldn't have provided us with a clitoris.

In fact I couldn't have had a worse role model in Mum as far as celebrating womanhood was concerned. Like most Fellowship women, she took pride in her appearance, adjusting her headscarf and hair clips until they looked perfect, demonstrating her devotion to God. But dressing for beauty's sake, or to please my dad, didn't come into it. And, following the move, she became withdrawn, and positively nasty to Dad.

One Saturday morning Dad woke up and announced that, as it was a sunny day, we'd have a day trip to the Isle of Wight. Since we weren't attending meetings, and didn't have to be back early in the evening, our excursions had become almost ridiculously long.

Usually, the excitement would start the night before, when Dad would disappear up the ladder into the attic, Mum standing below calling instructions up to him. He'd reappear with the cool box and lower it carefully down to her. This was a sure sign that we were going on a seriously long day trip.

We'd leave at the crack of dawn, and sometimes before the sun was up. Mum would come in to my and Samantha's bedrooms and gently shake us awake. I always shot out of bed, ready for adventure, but Samantha would roll back to sleep as soon as Mum had left her room.

Downstairs the kitchen would be in a chaotic state, food spread out on every available worktop space. If I'm honest, I wasn't too bothered about where we were going, more what I would be eating while we went there. We'd take breakfast with us, as it was too early to eat anything more than a cereal bar, which I munched on while Mum bustled around preparing sandwiches.

The cool box would be loaded to the top with the sandwiches, sausage rolls, pork pies, homemade coleslaw, crisps and homemade cakes. Last, Mum would fill large flasks with tea and coffee and pack them in a bag. It was Dad's job to load the stuff in the car, and this could take anywhere between thirty minutes and an hour, as he'd pack and repack everything several times, moaning, 'Edith, why do we have to take so much stuff?'

Before he'd even think about doing this, however, he'd spend a good amount of time doing all his car safety checks: tyre pressure, oil level, petrol. On and on the list went. Meanwhile, I'd be hopping up and down impatiently, desperate to leave. My mind was focused on the hard-boiled eggs and sausages we'd be stopping off to eat on the way.

Sometimes we even took a little camping stove and fried the sausages in the open air. Dad was never satisfied to pull over at the side of the road somewhere, but would have done detailed research to find the most scenic picnic sites.

Eventually he would be ready to go, the car bulging with all the bags of food, deckchairs, rugs, swim suits, changes of shoes, camera, binoculars, and anything else Mum thought of to weigh the car down.

Samantha and I would settle into our seats, with our books and magazines to read. Mum would do a last-minute dash to the toilet, and leave us waiting for another ten minutes. Inevitably, as we pulled away up the road, Samantha would emerge from her daydream and enquire, 'Have you got my walking boots?' With a groan, Mum would say, 'But I thought you had them,' while Dad reversed back up to the house.

On this particular day, however, the cool box hadn't been brought down from the attic, instead, sandwiches were being packed into three small lunch boxes. The atmosphere in the house was frosty. It turned out that Mum wasn't going to come with us to the Isle of Wight. This did concern me somewhat. Who would make sure that I was fed regularly? Dad was extremely organized, but I didn't trust him to know when it was snack time. I accepted that Mum wasn't coming with us, but found it odd, as we always did everything together. But, despite Dad's pleadings with her to change her mind, she didn't. Instead she kissed me and Samantha goodbye and swiftly sidestepped Dad's hug.

Things weren't the same without Mum to chat to. On the ferry across to the Isle of Wight Samantha was her usual dreamy self. Dad looked out to sea, whistling softly under his breath and only occasionally, when he remembered that we were there, turning to check we were all right. Although it was quiet without Mum, we managed to have a nice time. We rode the cable car up the cliff with candy floss in our mouths. Days out with Dad weren't that bad, I thought.

Dad even remembered to give us our lunch. He opened the first lunchbox and picked out a tomato. 'Who wants one?' he asked. I pointed out that there were three boxes which meant there was probably one for each of us, and therefore we didn't need to share one tomato between the three of us. Sure enough, each tub contained its own tomato, as well as sandwiches and a packet of crisps. I don't know why, but Dad's mistake on that day haunted me for a long time afterwards. Every time I thought of it I got hot all over with embarrassment.

I was really looking forward to getting home and seeing Mum. We turned into the drive at dinnertime and I burst in through the front door, shouting for her. I ran from room to room searching until I found her in the dining room. She was sitting in her favourite armchair, knitting. She looked up as we all came into the room, chatting excitedly. She didn't say anything, but carried on poking her needles in and out of the wool on her lap, which was rapidly shaping into another cardigan.

'Any chance of some dinner, Edith?' Dad said. Still without a word, she got up and went into the kitchen. She clattered around for a few minutes, then returned with two plates of tuna-fish pie, and set them down in front of me and Samantha. Dad waited a moment then called out, 'Is there any for me?' Mum came in and looked at him, then uttered her first word since we got home. 'No.' Dad thought she was joking and laughingly said, 'Edith!' She wasn't laughing, though.

Dad ate a boiled egg that night for his dinner. It was the only thing he knew how to cook. Mum came and sat down with us at Dad's request, but didn't say anything more. She didn't eat anything either. I think the strain of our situation and the isolation was starting to get Mum down, and she took it out on Dad. For a while after the Isle of Wight trip, although Mum started cooking for Dad again, she often didn't eat anything herself. I'd never seen anyone not eat their food before.

Chapter Sixteen

Tailor Me, Dummy

As the years went by and the call from the Fellowship that we were expecting failed to materialize, Mum and Dad gradually made small concessions in Fellowship rules. They had no choice, really. In order to continue to live our life of total seclusion, compromises had to be made, but I was under no illusions. The concessions did not mean that we weren't still aspiring to be Fellowship members again, one day.

After Mum started working and I had started at the new school, it became impossible for me to come home for my lunch, as the break was only three-quarters of an hour long. We tried it once, but, by the time Mum had picked me up and taken me home, it was time to dash back. Mum and Dad didn't make much of an issue of me having to eat at school, they just decided that it would be the best thing under the circumstances.

I had a stern warning from Mum, telling me to stay separate from the other kids while I ate. However, I was given no other advice about how I might actually carry this out. I never even attempted to sit apart.

At school I had become friends with a lovely girl called Lisa. She was tall, big-built and bubbly. While the other girls presented their newly emerging interest in sex for all the boys to see, Lisa just carried on being herself, and boys fell in love with her. I don't know how it was done, but she was surrounded by boys wherever she went. And I followed in her wake. My confidence had grown since I'd thrown off Kimberly and her pal, Eve, and being friends with Lisa strengthened it even more. I felt safe in her shadow, shielded by her normality.

We were different in a lot of ways, but we did share one thing: a love of food.

Most of the kids ate out in the playground when the weather was nice, and, when it was not, they went inside to their classrooms. I took a packed lunch with me and ate with Lisa and Stephanie. Before long they were looking forward to my lunch as much as I did. Mum always put in a sausage roll or pork pie, and this attracted a great deal of attention. It seemed that worldly people didn't eat these delicious foods as often as I did. Soon I was sharing my lunch with my friends. I'd break off pieces of pastry and hand them around.

Lisa and I began collecting pennies that we found on the ground and started the 'Snickers Fund'. Every day we'd count our findings and when we had twenty-one pence we'd buy our favourite treat at the tuck shop and share it between the two of us.

Nothing bad happened, and the sky didn't fall down on me.

When we got home from school I would phone Lisa, telling Mum that we had to share notes about our homework. Not much work got done, as we used this time to discuss Lisa's latest catch, in minute detail. I never mentioned my fantasies and I certainly never told her whom I fancied. I was becoming more adept at hiding my thoughts and feelings from people, both at school and at home.

One thing that Lisa couldn't protect me from was school non-uniform days. Nothing came close to the dread I felt about these events, not even the trip to Wales when I was at primary school. While everyone else cheered when we were told we were to have a day of wearing our own clothes, I felt myself go cold with fear.

The only previous occasion when I'd had to wear my home clothes to school was when we did a sponsored walk. This was the first time I had ever taken part in any charity event, and found out that I was expected to ask people to donate their hard-earned cash, if I completed the course. This in itself presented a major problem. I had no one to ask except my parents!

I was very tempted to make up some plausible names and sacrifice my pocket money but, in the end, Mum and Dad took the form to work with them and asked their colleagues to sponsor me. This was a good start, but I still looked at my form anxiously.

'What if I don't have enough names and my classmates see that I have no friends?' I fretted, but I needn't have worried. Most of the kids had forgotten to get any sponsors at all. My cover had not been blown.

The day of the walk came and I got dressed, still feeling deeply anxious. I put on my favourite purple skirt, a T-shirt and my sensible walking shoes and hoped that would do. But when I got to school I was made painfully aware that I'd overlooked some sort of unwritten rule. 'You're wearing a skirt' was the first comment thrown at me as I walked into the classroom. Everyone stared at me, and I wanted the floor to swallow me up. 'Yeah, I like skirts. They're easier to walk in,' I drily replied. I experienced similar comments the whole day, but kept my cheerful smile glued to my face at all times. Just to make sure, I cracked jokes and skipped along with the other kids, all the while praying that I would never, ever again have to go to school in my Fellowship clothes.

Unfortunately, the time came when that was exactly what I had to do, and yet again Mum refused to help me out of the tricky situation. 'Please, Mum,' I begged when she refused to let me stay off school 'sick' on non-uniform day. She stayed firm in her answer but agreed that I could look through the Great Universal clothing catalogue to find something I could buy especially for the day that loomed. I searched every page and every cover for something suitable, but all the clothes were either meant for older ladies or were skirts that were too short – or they were trousers. I spent nights tossing and turning, worrying about how I could remedy the situation. In my dreams I was a beautiful girl in dresses so wonderful that everyone envied me. In reality, I was a frump.

Eventually, after trying on everything in my wardrobe several times on the morning of the dreaded day, I settled on a long denim pinafore dress. This, I thought, was at least in fashion. Indeed it was, but the only other person being 'fashionable' was my Spanish teacher. 'Nice dress,' she grinned at me as I went into her class.

My luck seemed to be turning at last. The mid-nineties saw a change in clothing for girls. Suddenly it was trendy to wear long maxi-skirts, and I finally began to look more like one of the worldly girls. Overlooking the transitory nature of fashion, I bought enough of this kind of skirt to last me till the day I died. Red ones, denim ones, ones with buttons down the front – the list was endless. I thought I had gone to skirt heaven.

The Fellowship women must have been relieved, too, I suspect. I saw them around sometimes, identifiable by their headscarves and long hair, but I didn't recognize any of them from the meetings. Six years had passed since we had been 'withdrawn from', and I felt as removed from them as I did the rest of the world. To them, without a scarf on my head I was just like every other worldly girl.

I couldn't help but notice that every single one of the young Fellowship women started wearing denim skirts, too. Cowards, I thought. They must be so ashamed of their religion if they feel that they need to blend in with the worldly people.

I considered myself a special case, of course. I needed to fit in because I didn't have the privilege of being in the Fellowship, and the security that came with that. These girls were lucky enough to have the Fellowship, but looked as though they didn't want it. It made me feel even prouder of my Mum and Samantha, who had never given up wearing their Fellowship garb.

I found that kind of pride harder to feel when I was out with them among worldly people, though.

Chapter Seventeen

Seafood

We took to going on holiday frequently, sometimes two or three times a year. I think Mum and Dad must have suddenly found they had quite a pool of money accumulating now that they weren't putting it in a little tin every Sunday.

Our first holiday was to Cornwall. We stayed in a static caravan on a campsite in Bude and I felt as if the world and his wife must be looking at us. We arrived prepared, as usual, with everything that we might need, not just for a day this time, but an entire two weeks. This meant we had a lot of stuff. In fact, so much stuff that Dad had bought a roof box to go on the car, especially for the purpose of transporting it all.

Under the watchful eyes of people in neighbouring caravans we began the mammoth job of carrying everything from the car to our temporary home. At last every single item had been removed from the top box, the boot, the foot wells of the seats and the back seat itself. I looked at it all. On the tiny dining table were several cardboard boxes, all filled with enough store-cupboard items to feed the four of us for a week. We weren't allowed to eat out, so going to a restaurant or café wasn't an option for us. If we felt really daring we might buy fish and chips from the local chip shop, the best day of the holiday as far as Samantha and I were concerned.

Before we began to unpack there was one thing that had to be done. Mum hunted through boxes and bags until she found what she was looking for. Triumphantly, she held up a tea towel. Clambering over suitcases she made straight for the television set that sat on a shelf, in the seating area of the caravan. She shook out the towel and carefully hung it over the TV screen, securing it with a fruit bowl. Now we could all relax. The Devil wasn't welcome in this caravan, and the tea towel ensured that God knew this.

The caravan site was crawling with boys. Samantha and I spent every spare moment staring at them from behind the net curtains of the caravan window, deciding which ones we fancied. Late one afternoon, while Mum was preparing a meat pie from a can, tinned potatoes, tinned peas and tinned carrots for our dinner, I washed my hair, which was salty from a day of swimming in the sea. Samantha and Dad were reading, and, as I sat on the steps of the caravan brushing out my long hair, I let myself imagine that I was allowed to have a boyfriend. Before long I was lost in my own world, dreaming of love and romance.

'Dinner's ready, Lindsey,' Mum called. 'I hope you're ready.'

'Ready' of course meant having my hair tied back with a token in. I slowly pulled the hair band off my wrist, where I kept it for handiness, and fastened it back in my hair. Suddenly I really wished that there weren't so many damned rules.

Chapter Eighteen

Camping in Gurnsey

Samantha kept on and on about when our suffocating lifestyle was going to come to an end. Mum and Dad encouraged her to keep reading her Bible and pray, which she did obediently. This seemed only to add to her anxiety. 'Do you think we're wrong?' she'd ask Mum. What she meant was, 'Do you think the Fellowship were right to reject us?' I had heard Mum and Dad ask themselves the same question many, many times over the years, but to us they remained steadfast in their belief that we had done nothing wrong and certain members of the Fellowship had been corrupted by the Devil.

They continued to have faith that God would sort it all out. Doubt, however, was creeping into Samantha's mind and manifested itself as self-hatred.

A holiday helped alleviate the pressure. By this time we had explored just about every inch of the British Isles. Dad, in particular, had ambitions to go even further afield. He had a love of France and anything French. He had been taking evening classes at the local college, improving his schoolboy French. Mum, however, wasn't having any of it. 'We are most definitely not going abroad,' she stated firmly. Her main objection was that she didn't trust Dad to drive on the right-hand side of the road. Dad was crushed, but came up with the next-best thing. 'Let's go to the Channel Islands, then,' he suggested. I think he thought he might be able to at least see France from there on a clear day.

Finding suitable accommodation proved tricky. Cottages were too expensive, and hotels, of course, were out of the question. Mum and Dad discovered that on Guernsey there were camp sites that had ready-erected tents, and they reserved one for us in the summer of 1995.

Guernsey was beautiful. Long, empty beaches with golden sand stretched for miles and miles around the coastline, and I felt able to relax away from the scrutiny of the world. We spent lazy days, swimming and going for long rambles. Dad even persuaded Mum to let us go on a day trip to France, and we took the ferry over to Saint-Malo. I sensed that Mum and Dad were relaxing, too, and I was happy that they were happy. Mum was glad to find that the campsite had a kitchen that cooked an evening meal. Everyone took their own plates and the cooks piled them high with chilli con carne, jacket potatoes and vegetables. The meals were so huge that we felt stuffed when we had scraped every last bit of food into our mouths. Things felt good.

We arrived home after two weeks away. The first thing Mum and I did was weigh ourselves. I had taken to jumping on the scales, as I'd seen Mum frequently do, and I knew that I'd been ten stone before we went on holiday. I discovered that I was still the same weight and felt relieved. 'I guess all that swimming must have stopped those big dinners making us fat,' I commented to Mum.

Chapter Nineteen

Changing Appetites

I was well aware that I wasn't a stick insect, and kids at school weren't shy in coming forward with comments about my larger-than-average waistline. During an English lesson one day, we were put into pairs to work on a project. I hated being separated from Lisa, and didn't like these unexpected interruptions to my grand plan for anonymity. I would undoubtedly be required to speak to kids I usually went out of my way to avoid. I was glad to see that I had been put with James. He was popular, and had a big mouth on him, but I quite liked him, as he never said a bad word against anybody. We didn't get much done as he wasn't particularly conscientious about working hard, but I kept my head down and did my best to write something to fob the teacher off. I became aware that James's eyes were on me, and I looked up. He put his head on one side, and said, 'You could lose some weight if you wanted, Lindsey.' He then added, 'Hayley did, and she looks really good.' I looked over at Hayley, and wished she was dead.

Putting on weight had its advantages for me sometimes. Having spent the long summer holidays eating, reading and not doing much else, I discovered that my skirt from the term before didn't fit me. Mum took me to the school-uniform shop and I was measured up. 'You're a size sixteen,' the shop lady announced. I nearly fainted. I had got fat, I thought. The lady went away to find a grey skirt in a size sixteen, and I looked at myself in the mirror critically. She came back with a slight frown on her face. 'I'm afraid we only have the short ones in that size,' she said. I didn't dare look at Mum's face, but inside I was taking secret tiny leaps of ecstasy.

'I don't know …' Mum sounded doubtful. 'Are you sure you haven't got anything longer?' I crossed my fingers and waited.

'No,' said the lady firmly. And so I went home with my first short skirt, ever. I couldn't care less that it was drab and grey. It was short. When I got home I put it on, twirling in front of the mirror. In fact the hem line was only about an inch above my knee. But that, I thought, gazing at myself, is a good start.

My bubble of joy was burst shortly after that. 'I never knew legs looked like that when they squeeze together at the top,' said Kimberly one afternoon. We were in our history lesson and she was sitting opposite me at another desk. Her eyes were directed straight at my chunky thighs, which were exposed in my newly shortened skirt. A look of disgust was on her face, so I tried to squeeze my legs together more tightly, but the fat at the top of them made it impossible.

I wanted the earth to swallow me up, but I just smiled at her and got on with my work. I studied other girls' legs after that and noticed all the different shapes and sizes. In the chemistry lab one day a few of us had gathered during break time, waiting for the lesson to start. Two girls, Sharon and Abbie, were sitting on a desk, their legs swinging. They both had short skirts on, and both looked confident and relaxed. Sharon was a bigger girl than Abbie, and I noticed that her legs were a similar size to mine, and they too spread out, as Kimberly had noted mine did. Abbie's legs, however, were long and slim, and didn't spread at all. I looked at Sharon's legs again and felt sorry for her.

I started revising for my GCSE mock exams during the October half-term of 1995. I sat in the empty house by the gas fire in the dining room. Dad said it was too early in the year to have the central heating on, but it was chilly, so Mum told me to light the fire, but not to tell Dad.

I was a good student and had studied really hard over the last five years, and Mum and Dad made it clear to me that all their hopes to have at least one child who did well academically lay with me. I liked my school work and felt a massive sense of achievement when I got good grades.

I looked at all the books spread out on the floor around me, but suddenly the prospect of poring over them all seemed tedious and tiresome. My thoughts turned to food. I wandered into the kitchen and had a rummage through the cupboards. My eyes came to rest on a tin in the larder. This was Mum's supply of Ryvita.

I took the tin from the shelf and opened the lid, sniffing the contents. The rectangular biscuits were the colour of cardboard and spattered with bird seed, and didn't look that appetizing, but I took one out and nibbled at the corner. It was dry but didn't taste as bad as it looked and smelled. I put a couple on a plate and looked around the kitchen.

I spotted a bowl of fresh tomatoes, and cut a cross in the top of one of them. Then I put the kettle on. I poured the boiling water over the fruit and, after a minute, the skin peeled off easily. I squeezed the tomato between my fingers. It was slimy on the outside, but still firm on the inside. After a few seconds in the microwave it had become a liquid mess. 'This is better,' I thought, and spread the tomato mush on the Ryvita. I carried my plate back to the dining room, settled back on the floor and began to read my books.

Chapter Twenty

Original Thin

There was frantic knocking on the bathroom door, but I
ignored it for a while.

'Lindsey,' Mum called. 'What are you doing? Come out so
I can see you.'

I wiped my mouth on a tissue, and flushed the toilet. I
watched the contents of my stomach swirl around the bowl
for a second or two before it disappeared. I lifted the seat of
the toilet and carefully cleaned the porcelain, wiping away all
traces of my activities.

At last I opened the door. Mum was still standing outside,
looking concerned. 'What were you doing in there?' she
asked again. 'I thought I heard you being sick.'

I shrugged my shoulders. 'No, I just needed a big poo.
Sorry to take so long,' I replied.

'Ninety-nine, one hundred ...' I fell on my back exhausted. I
pulled my feet out from under the piano stool, which had
held me in position while I did my daily routine of sit-ups.
When I had got my breath back I ran upstairs to the

bathroom and stepped gingerly on the scales. I was satisfied with the number I saw the needle bounce round to.

'You're looking good, Lindsey,' Mum commented to me a few weeks later. 'I should think that, now you've lost a bit of weight, your brain is at its optimum. That should help you get good results in your exams.'

That evening, after dinner, I excused myself from the table and made my way upstairs to the bathroom. While Mum and Dad washed up and chatted in the kitchen, and Samantha played her keyboard or read her Bible, I vomited up the food Mum had prepared and cooked for me. I didn't think twice about doing it. It had become part of my routine and suited me surprisingly well. After my usual check of my weight on the scales, I opened the bathroom door.

'I know what you're doing.' Mum stood there, her hands on her hips.

'I don't know what you mean,' I protested, and tried to push past her and go into my room.

'I know you're making yourself sick. It's not a good idea,' she said. 'Please don't, Lindsey.'

I looked at her and felt close to tears. What on earth had I been doing? I suddenly felt frightened that I was capable of doing something so abnormal without feeling bad about it. And I had lied to her.

'You're right,' I said softly. 'I *am* making myself sick.'

'Oh, Lindsey.' Mum put her arms around me. 'Oh, Lindsey,' she repeated stroking my head. She pushed me away so she could look at my face. 'You won't do it again, will you?'

'No,' I replied. And I honestly meant it.

I kept my promise but the compulsion to lose weight didn't leave me. Instead, I decided to cut down on the amount and the type of food that I was eating. I replaced Rice Krispies, smothered with sugar and hot milk in the morning, with a fat-free fromage frais. At lunchtime I swapped my pork-pie-and-egg sandwiches for a piece of cucumber cut so thin that I could see through it, sandwiched between two fat-free crackers.

'Don't overdo it, Lindsey,' my classmate Wayne said one day as he saw me lift the crackers to my mouth and take a tiny nibble. What he didn't know was that I wouldn't even eat all of it. I had taken to the habit of never finishing my meals. If I left something on my plate, or threw the last bit of my lunch away, then I felt good about myself. The trouble was, it soon got to the point where I was throwing it all away without eating any of it.

'Do eat something else, dear,' Dad said to me one morning. We were the only ones up. I had taken to getting up at six thirty a.m., the time that he had been rising for as long as I could remember. While he raided through the biscuit tin, and paced up and down the long galley kitchen, I dipped my teaspoon in my yoghurt pot and took tiny sips of the thin, fat-free liquid. When he went to wake Mum with a cup of tea in bed, I left the house and began the long walk up to Adeyfield and back. This wasn't so much a pleasant morning amble, intended to clear away the cobwebs, as a march, set at punishing pace, designed to burn off the few calories I had just consumed.

At school one day, Lisa called me 'Ana', referring to my anorexic appearance. Her concern for me was obvious, but I didn't rise to her overt attempt to engage me in a conversation about my changing body shape. Instead, I looked across the classroom at Kimberly, who was flirting with her latest conquest. That morning I had hit the eight-stone mark, and

I felt incredibly smug knowing that I weighed one stone less than my arch enemy.

Despite the steady weight loss, I didn't feel satisfied. I wanted to lose more, faster. My exercise routine had become impossible to maintain. I lacked energy, and protruding bones made it too painful. I broke my promise to Mum without much thought, and started making regular trips to the bathroom, not just after dinner, but after every meal. I couldn't stand the thought of any amount of food left in my body, and purged to rid myself of it all.

After six months of this regime I looked like a different person. The glasses I wore everywhere seemed ridiculously oversized on my fleshless face. My skin, almost translucent, hung taut over my protruding cheekbones, while the large, round, wire frames of my spectacles only served to accentuate the sunken hollows of my cheeks. My face and body had conveniently grown a film of downy fur in an attempt to shield my skeleton from the bitter winter cold. Unfortunately, my nose had no such protection and maintained a pinky red colour wherever I went. This got me nick-named 'Rudolph' by the kids at school. Mum sent me to school with a note to the teacher requesting that I could keep my coat on in the classroom. But, no matter how many clothes I wore, I couldn't get warm.

Sitting down had become agony. I would rock from one side of my skinny bum to the other, distributing the pain evenly, being careful not to jar the base of my spine in the process.

In front of the wall of mirrors in Samantha's bedroom, I inspected my body with meticulous care. I checked to see that my hip bones stood proud and that the outline of my rib cage was still visible. I measured the circumference of the tops of my legs by placing my two thumbs and middle fingers together, forming a ring around the femur.

My periods had stopped, but I didn't care. Nor did I care when my hair came out in thick clumps when I brushed it. Mum picked up handfuls of it from my bedroom floor, and said, 'Look what you're doing to yourself.' I ignored her, and tied back what was left with my hair band.

My head was a mess on the inside as well as the outside. I didn't think about anything but losing more and more weight. I went to sleep at night thinking about it, and was still thinking about it when I woke up in the morning.

The day of my first GCSEs arrived. It was French oral, and I had practised like mad, chatting in French with Dad, who was only too pleased to have an excuse to use the language he loved. I entered the classroom where I had sat for the last two years, preparing for this day.

My teacher, Mrs Tomlinson, told me to sit down opposite her. On the desk between us was a tape recorder, which, having prepped me on what to expect during the exam, she switched on. Smiling at me, she nodded encouragingly, and indicated for me to begin. My mind was blank. No words. Nothing. I laid my head on the desk and felt my limbs go limp. Weighing five stone ten pounds, my body gave in.

I was taken to my local general practitioner, who wrote a letter to the school, telling them that I was unfit to continue my education. I had nothing to show for my years of hard work. I felt as if I had thrown it all away.

Chapter Twenty-One

Jekyll and Hyde

I spent the long days at home on my own. I didn't have the concentration to read any more so Mum and Dad said I could get story cassettes from the library. I listened to them on Dad's Walkman which he had bought when he started subscribing to *La Vie Outre-Manche*, a French magazine for people living in Britain.

The magazine came with cassettes, and in true Dad style, not wanting to miss one single iota of information, he had brought the Walkman. I sat at the dining room table, doing jigsaw puzzles and listening to Charles Dickens and Thomas Hardy. In the afternoons when Mum came home from work, we played Scrabble, and, despite my malnourished mind, I beat her at every single game. After each contest she groaned and said, 'I don't know why I bother.' To make matters worse for her, I did the *Telegraph* cryptic crossword while she had her go in the Scrabble game, and didn't even *look* at my letters until it was my turn.

I visited the doctor every week. When I stood on his scales, he told me how much I weighed, and told me to eat more. I said I'd try, but had no intention of doing so.

This routine continued for a few weeks, until one night I woke up suddenly. I felt different somehow, and sat up in bed in the dark, trying to work out what it was. Then it hit me. I was hungry, absolutely famished. My stomach was churning with the desire for food. I got out of bed and stumbled into Mum's bedroom.

'Mum,' I whispered hoarsely. 'Mum, wake up.'

She came to and shot up in bed. 'What is it?' She looked really scared.

'Don't worry Mum,' I said. 'It's good news. I feel hungry.'

And good news is what I thought it was. Months had passed since I'd last felt any yearning for food, my stomach having shrunk so much that the feeling of hunger had deserted me, making it even harder to convince my twisted mind that I should put food in my mouth.

'I want to eat, now,' I said. I felt desperate. Desperate to satisfy this feeling that was ravishing my body.

I could tell that Mum was a little disturbed by this sudden turn of events, and not quite sure how to respond, but I gave her no time to hesitate as I hurried her into her dressing gown. We both went downstairs to the kitchen. 'What do you want to eat, then?' Mum asked. I stood in the middle of the room flanked on both sides by cupboards and shelves laden with food. Delicious, delicious food.

My mind felt as if it would burst. The desire to eat was overwhelming and I couldn't think straight. 'A tin of beans with little sausages in,' I blurted out.

Mum looked a bit dubious. 'Are you sure? It's the middle of the night, you know.'

'Oh, all right.' I didn't care at that moment. Anything would do. 'You make me something,' I said.

I ate the muesli and milk that she gave me, and asked for more. I kept eating until I felt as if I would pop. I went back to bed, and settled down to sleep feeling happy for the first time in months. I'm getting better, I thought as I drifted off to sleep. I'm really getting better.

The next morning, however, I felt differently.

I woke up in a foul mood. Standing in front of the mirror, I pinched my stomach, squeezing the thin skin between my fingers. I felt revulsion for the person I saw looking back at me. The food I had eaten in the night showed itself in my protruding belly, which was usually concave.

Suddenly I felt consumed by rage. It welled up inside me, wave after wave, engulfing my mind in a blackness that I had never felt before. I began thumping my fist against the side of my head over and over again, pain searing through my skull. The throbbing helped ease the vile accusations of greed and failure that my mind was screaming at me, and I stopped. Feeling calmer, I got dressed, and went downstairs. 'I think I'm going to get better, Mum,' I said. 'I'm going to be normal again.'

The next few weeks were the worst of my life. I swung between an all-consuming desire for food, and absolute abhorrence for myself. When everyone left the house I raided the freezer, getting out packs of sausage rolls, cheese-and-onion pies, fish fingers and pizza. I prepared them with my fingers trembling as I ripped open the packets, desperate to get at the food. I'd eat it all, feeling high, almost delirious with the adrenalin rushing through my body, and then lie on the floor feeling ill.

I tried, really tried, to stop my mind hating me for breaking the rules that I had so carefully put in place to control my life over the past few months. But I couldn't. It was too much for me to bear. So my solution was to purge my body of the pollutant. I vomited until my stomach was empty, and my throat was sore. I was so used to making myself sick now that all I had to do was clench my tummy muscles and the entire contents of my stomach would reappear.

Now I felt really scared. Putting on weight was a real possibility, because I was eating again. I binged on a daily basis, deliberately starving myself during the day knowing that I was going to eat a day's worth of food in one sitting during the evening meal. But, even though I knew I would do this, all through the day I would tell myself that tonight I wouldn't; tonight would be different. I was like Jekyll and Hyde. One part of me wanted to look after myself; the other taunted me for having the desire to eat and be well. I felt at the mercy of both.

The need to monitor my weight was compulsive and obsessive, and I went nowhere without Mum's scales. In 1996 the four of us travelled on holiday to Scotland. It was a long drive and I slept most of the way, my head on Samantha's soft lap. At last we arrived in a tranquil Scottish village. I hurriedly unpacked my suitcase and took out the weighing scales that I had sneaked in there before we left. I put them on the floor and quickly stepped on. Feeling anxious, I peered at the needle. I was so scared that my lack of activity during the car journey might have meant I'd put on weight. Mum poked her head around the bedroom door, and guiltily I tried to shove them back in my case. The disappointment on her face was clear. 'I thought you were going to leave the scales at home,' she said. I had promised her that I would. In fact, I had promised *myself* that I would. But that's what my life was like then, a lot of promises made, which I felt unable to keep, and which were broken before the day was over.

The cycle of bingeing and purging took its toll on me and I became deeply depressed. I felt as if someone had tossed a heavy blanket over me, and I couldn't throw it off. The doctor offered me the antidepressant drug Prozac, but I refused to take it, still believing that I could win the battle on my own without resorting to medical help. Mum didn't leave me at home on my own any more. She didn't trust me not to do something stupid, and thought I might end up killing myself. The thought never crossed my mind. First, I knew I wouldn't get to Heaven if I did and, second, I didn't stop believing that I would get well.

I started going to work with Mum, helping out with little jobs around the office. With this security, and Mum's constant encouragement, I managed to put on a stone in weight over the summer. I decided I was well enough to go back to school, and wanted to have another go at my GCSEs. My school were delighted to welcome me back, the teachers and kids happy at my apparent recovery. But my improved physical appearance hid the real story. They had no idea of the turmoil in my head, and I didn't tell them.

The plan was that I would study for my GCSEs, while also beginning my A-levels. It came as a complete shock when my parents agreed that I could go into higher education. I had asked them if I could, because I was desperate for something else to think about and occupy my mind, other than relentless thoughts of food and weight. By then they were ready to say yes to anything I asked for, even if it was something forbidden by the Fellowship. They just wanted me to be well.

The risks that higher education posed must have seemed a small price to pay for their daughter's health. Besides, they were expecting the Fellowship to call with their pardon any day, and that would put a stop to it.

Mum even agreed to let me take riding lessons, which I'd dreamt of as a child.

'If I get up to six stone in the next month, can I have horse-riding lessons?' I asked.

She thought for a moment, probably weighing up how much this would cost, before making me an offer 'Wouldn't you rather have a new pair of shoes?'

I sensed her desperation, and held out for the lessons.

As hard as I tried, I couldn't reach the target weight, but no one was prepared to risk upsetting me more, so I was given a new pair of shoes as well as riding lessons.

Best of all, I even got to wear jodhpurs. In any other circumstances, mum would never agree to me wearing anything other than a long skirt. I felt almost worldly, dressed in trousers, acceptably thin, to my mind, riding around like a normal girl.

The sad thing was, my arms had become too weak to hold the reins, I lacked the strength to squeeze the horse's flanks with my thighs, and there was no flesh left on my pelvis to protect it from the agonizing bumping up and down in the saddle. I only lasted a few lessons before it got too much.

My big plans for my education also fell apart all too soon. I found the task I had been set was impossible. I hadn't even read a book since I'd been at home, and struggled to focus my attention on anything but the constant monologues that went on in my head. I left school again, but, still determined to get myself some qualifications, enrolled at college. I settled in well, and didn't feel the same agony of being different that I had felt at school. This was largely due to two things: first, my thinness had made me feel acceptable to the worldly world; and, second, I was in a permanent state of disconnection from everyone, trapped in my head.

Victor gave me some money for my seventeenth birthday. In my card he wrote, 'For driving lessons, not shoes!' He needn't have worried. I couldn't wait to learn to drive.

I imagined Mum would be the best person to sit with me while we bunny hopped down the road, but after our first trip out together she point blank refused to get back in the car with me until I had passed my test.

The job was given to Dad, which I wasn't too pleased about. Dad and I didn't spend much time together and I wondered what we'd talk about. I needn't have worried. Dad wasn't much of a talker, and we usually drove in silence, with him occasionally asking, 'Are you all right dear?' He showed me how to hold the head rest on the front passenger seat when reversing, and I gently broke the news that the manoeuvre wasn't recognized by the test centre. He surprised me with his ability to remain calm when I stalled in the middle of the road on a steep hill with a lorry bearing down on us, and I surprised myself when I realized that I had enjoyed our drives together.

I took lessons with a crazy Irish bloke who chewed gum and talked incessantly. He'd tell me to turn left and wrench the wheel from me with a sharp rebuke when I steered to the right. I had never felt so free in my life, temporarily released from the claustrophobia at home and the tortuous thoughts of self-hatred and disgust for my body. The hour-long lessons were over all too soon.

My test took place in a nearby town and we left the test centre in the car just as it began to snow. It wasn't until the exam was nearly over that I realized I hadn't put the car lights on. With a sinking feeling I switched them on as I turned back into the test centre car park. I mumbled that I thought visibility was getting bad, and that it was time to put the lights on, but I felt like I had blown it. Perhaps the examiner hadn't noticed the dark conditions either, because he announced that I had passed my test.

When I got home I immediately asked Mum if I could go out for a drive in her car. She had a little Fiat Uno, which I had practised in. Mum reluctantly agreed that I could take her car out, with a warning to be careful as she needed it for work the next day. Before I went I sneaked upstairs and, standing on Mum's dressing table stool, I reached to the back of the wardrobe where I knew Dad kept his Walkman. I took it, and grabbed some *La Vie Outre-Manche* cassette tapes. With these safely hidden in my bag, I got in the car. I knew exactly which tape I was looking for, having played it many times before, just not in a car. I put the selected cassette in the Walkman, wound it on to the right spot, put the ear plugs in, and drove off. I might not have a radio in the car, but I did have a female singer blasting French pop songs into my ears.

At last, I didn't have to take the bus anymore. The car became my own private space, in which I could be myself, free from the expectations of the two worlds I was caught between.

Chapter Twenty-Two

I Can't Do It On My Own

I spent two years at college. During the first I completed my GCSEs, and in the second I began my A-levels. I had started working, too. During the summer holidays I did temping, and on the first day of the break I got a call asking me to work in the paper samples office at Sappi Graphics Paper Mill.

The mill was a two-minute walk from my house, so ideally located for me to come home for lunch. I wasn't so much concerned about keeping myself separate from worldly people as not eating in front of people because of my strange eating habits. I ate the same food every day, because this made me feel safe and in control. And I was still making myself sick if I had a binge, which was most days. But that wasn't all. I had also begun a stranger habit, which I didn't want anyone to know about, least of all a mill full of people.

I had discovered that I liked regurgitating my food into my mouth. If I drank exactly the right amount of water with my meal I could bring the food back up, which I'd then roll around my tongue and swallow again. I'd do this several times until only bile came up, and I felt as if I had found the secret to staying slim, while still eating as much as I wanted. Unfortunately, the regurgitated meal would sometimes come up with such force that it dribbled down my chin and splattered on the front of my clothes. There was no way I could risk this happening, so I decided to take the job and lunch at home.

The agency had said I would be needed for only one day, but I ended up working there the whole summer, and being offered a permanent position. I didn't take it, though, as I wanted to continue my education, and I was also terrified that if I stayed they would discover what a terrible job I was doing. I was only seventeen years old and found out only a couple of minutes after entering the office that I was totally out of my depth. 'Should I answer that?' I asked timidly when the telephone rang. It was confirmed to me by the woman who worked on reception that, as I was the only person now working in the office, yes, I should.

I spent the summer taking requests for paper samples, which I spent hours trying to find in the huge depot. I dispatched boxes of paper when I should have sent one or two sheets, and I misunderstood the packaging system, probably costing the mill thousands of pounds. All things considered, I decided the best thing was to leave.

During my second year at college my weight plummeted again. By the end of the year I was back down to six stone. The fact was, quite simply, that I couldn't cope with having flesh on my body. I couldn't see the skeletal figure that other people saw, and I was continually striving to lose weight. But

I still wanted to be well, and that was my problem. I still had the two voices of Jekyll and Hyde in my head, which never rested, both giving me conflicting sets of instructions. I felt compelled to follow both of them, and it exhausted me.

My serious physical state made it impossible for me to return to college for a third year, so I left. My doctor referred me to the local hospital, where I had regular blood tests. I also had a bone scan, which revealed that I was in the early stages of osteoporosis. I knew that this was serious, and the doctors continually lectured me about the long-term effects of being underweight.

They told me that I would probably become infertile, that my brittle bones would break, I might go blind and my heart could give out any moment. I understood, but felt helpless. I was living very much in the moment, and looking to the future only made me feel worse.

As far as I was concerned, I had no proper future. I was in a living hell, which was the state of being 'withdrawn from'. I was eighteen years old, and had no hope of an education, a career or marriage.

Mum got a new job at the General Hospital, and I went with her every day. I sat next to her at her desk, with my knees pressed up against the drawers. I watched her laugh and chat with people in the office and realized that she too had adapted to our secluded life by allowing herself to behave like two different people. Her desk was next to Dora's, who read tarot cards, smoked heavily and was as worldly as they come. Mum and Dora got on like a house on fire.

I was given the job of sorting the medical records into piles, ready for when the consultants saw the patients. This kind of monotonous work suited me, and the voices in the large office, buzzing around me, helped drown out the voices in my head.

The hardest part of the day was when it was time to eat. We'd open our packed lunches at Mum's desk. I brought my ready-prepared sandwich, cut up into cubes. I had to sit on my hands while Mum popped the little square blocks into my mouth, kindly doing so when no one was looking. At home, everyone was used to it, but it wasn't something Mum or I wanted to share with the office. There certainly wasn't any way I could feed myself. If I tried, I became uncontrollably enraged, and punched myself in the jaw. My obsession with losing weight had become so extreme that I wanted to punish myself for needing to eat. I saw it as a weakness. It became clear to both Mum and me that preventive measures had to be taken after I stabbed the side of my face with my fork.

In order to get past my all-consuming anger, I felt the only thing I could do was to con my mind into thinking that I wasn't really eating, so Mum and I came up with ways that I could do this. A few times we tried pushing the dinner table against the wall and serving buffet-style meals, the four of us wandering around the dining room, selecting food from dishes on the table. Dad and Samantha were mystified by what was going on, wondering where the usual meat and two veg had gone, but Mum just hissed at them to shut up, and they obeyed her.

It was really only Mum who understood the seriousness of my condition. Samantha was lost in her own world and Dad thought it was a simple case of my having to snap out of it and eat a good square meal. This attitude made me cling to Mum even more. She became my lifeline.

'You control my life,' Mum snapped one evening. 'You don't give me any time to myself.'

I felt as if my lifeline was severed. I crawled into bed, lay in the dark and hoped that I wouldn't wake up in the morning.

A phone call came out of the blue one day, and was the cause of great excitement in our household. The Fellowship had somehow heard that I was unwell, and wanted to send some representatives to the house to speak to us all.

Mum and Dad dared to hope that the visit was for the purpose of finally welcoming them back into the Fellowship. It was hard to imagine what else it might be about.

When the day came, two priests arrived at our door, and were warmly invited in. We all assembled in the front room, and the men sat on the two-seater sofa in front of the window. I felt so privileged that priests of the Fellowship had made a special visit out of concern for me.

After the pleasantries were over, one of the priests, Mr Bronson, told us how his own daughter had suffered from anorexia.

'I know what you're going through,' he said. 'She's recovered, thankfully. We want you to know that we will carry on praying for your swift recovery.'

And that was it, they were off. It was not what Mum and Dad had been desperately hoping to hear for the past eleven years.

The disappointing news had practical implications for our family too. As our wait continued, Dad was finding it harder and harder to maintain his Fellowship values at the worldly firm he worked for.

He was working at Davall Gears, designing gearboxes, but the industry was embracing new technology, and the company were pressurising him to use AutoCAD software for his technical drawings. It meant using a computer, and abandoning the drawing-board method altogether. The Fellowship strongly objected to their members using computers, although they were happy enough to employ worldly people to do so for them.

Dad didn't want to jeopardize our chances of going back, but Davall Gears were insistent that he moved with the times. Not wanting to leave his job, Dad agreed to train, but comforted himself with the thought that, when he got back to the Fellowship, he could leave and find a computer-free job within the fold.

Chapter Twenty-Three

So Near And Yet So Far

D ad lost all contact with his parents, two brothers and two sisters when we were 'withdrawn from'. They all lived somewhere in the area, so we occasionally saw them in the street from afar. I passed my Uncle Geoffrey's house every day on the way to college, as did Mum on her way to work, but all we could hope for was to get a fleeting glimpse of them in the garden, going about their business.

Just seeing them lifted our spirits and gave meaning to who we were and what we were hoping to become a part of again. If Uncle Geoffrey, Auntie Gail or their daughter Caroline, spotted us, they'd still give us a big smile and cheerful wave, but we resisted the temptation to wave back. They'd always been a little too 'worldly' for my parents' liking, and were breaking the rules by communicating with us in that way, but we obeyed the rules nonetheless. There was nothing else we could do, if we were to return to the Fellowship.

Caroline's brother, Leon, was married to Danielle and had a family of his own. I hadn't seen him since the Fellowship meetings, when I was seven years old, and knew almost nothing about his life since then.

I must have been seventeen when we found out the exciting news that Leon and his family had moved into a house just a few doors down the road from us. Mum and Dad forbade Samantha and me from talking to them, but it was inevitable that one of us would eventually come face to face with them in the street, and be left with no choice but to say hello.

Not being able to talk to them did not mean we couldn't watch them come and go, and we soon began to notice something strange about the way they looked and acted. Danielle was seen without a headscarf, wore trousers, and appeared to have cut her hair. I started volunteering to collect our weekly fish and chip meal from the take away so I could peer in their windows on the way past. And Mum took walks past their garden at the time that Fellowship meetings were scheduled and noticed that their car was still in the drive.

When we did eventually bump into one of the family, our suspicions were confirmed. They too were 'shut up'. They made it clear that they wanted to become friends, but Mum and Dad declined their offer, not wanting anything to compromise our quest for re-admittance into the Fellowship.

However, when it became obvious that I wasn't recovering from my anorexia, they reconsidered their options. Mum and Dad discussed the idea that Samantha and I might visit them, with a view that the companionship of Fellowship members, 'shut up' or otherwise, might help us both. Mum approached Danielle, who said that Samantha and I were welcome to visit her and the children at any time. It felt so strange going into their house. I hadn't been into the home of someone from the Fellowship since I was seven, so I felt like I was somehow breaking the rules. And yet my anxiety was mixed with relief at being amongst people who understood my values. I was confused, and the experience made me feel even more like I didn't belong anywhere.

What Mum didn't realize was Leon and Danielle had no intention of going back to the Fellowship. She took me out with her, running errands, and I saw the CD player she had in the car. Samantha found all this too much to cope with, so she didn't go to their house very often, but I stuck with it, desperate for the friendship. Danielle said to me that I should look beyond the boundaries of the Fellowship. She told me that Leon's mum and dad were 'shut up', too. They came to her house often, bringing Caroline, whom I had played with at the meetings. I felt I had nothing in common with these people, who were so scathing about the Fellowship, but they were the closest contact I had with it, so I smiled politely, and privately despised them.

She told me how she struggled with her own weight and dieted during the week, so she could eat what she wanted at the weekends. I started doing the same, only I ate virtually nothing during the week and swallowed a week's worth of food at the weekend, then purged my body of the whole lot.

Far from getting better, I became more depressed and eventually told Mum that I couldn't go on without professional help. Mum and Dad agreed to help me find it. After three years of absolute hell I thought at last there was light at the end of the tunnel.

Chapter Twenty-Four

A Clinical Decision

I didn't say much during the drive to Norwich. Instead I looked out of the window, and wondered what the future held for me. I had funding for six months at Newmarket House Clinic for Eating Disorders, and I knew I had to make the most of it. My instinct told me that this was the only opportunity I was going to have to get help for my anorexia.

When I was searching for information about eating disorders, I had found a book by a woman called Peggy-Claude Pierre. Peggy had set up the Montreux Clinic in Canada, which treated eating disorders, and the key, she said, to recovery was unconditional love. The idea made sense to me, and I clung to the hope that there might be a clinic in England that was based on the same kind of philosophy. I had already looked into the possibility of going to Rhodes Farm, but it was really for children and I was eighteen. My doctor had also mentioned the Maudsley Hospital in London, which was a psychiatric unit for adults.

But I needed somewhere where my mind could be treated as well as my body. When I found out about Newmarket

House Clinic I felt like all my dreams had come true. It too based its healing process on mending the mind, as well as the physical symptoms of anorexia.

I knew I had made the correct choice almost as soon as I arrived. The building was light and airy, with large rooms and simple decor. The heavy front door shut out the world and I felt protected and safe in the hands of loving staff.

I was introduced to my therapist, Diane, shortly after I arrived. I sat on the mattress in my new bedroom, and waited for the stranger who was going to help me sort my life out. I hadn't planned what to say to her, but I knew that I was going to be honest.

'I was born into the Fellowship, but we've been excommunicated, and I think that's what's making me ill,' I said before she had hardly sat down.

I had never so much as admitted this to myself before, let alone said the words out loud. In fact, the idea had been put into my head by a conversation I'd had with two psychologists who assessed me when I applied for funding to pay for my stay at the clinic.

'You're in the Fellowship,' the female shrink had stated.

I had been sitting in a small room, one of many offices belonging to Dacorum Borough Council. It felt claustrophobic and cluttered, and wasn't helped much by the fact there were three of us crammed together in the tiny space. I nodded in response to the question. My mouth felt dry because I was so nervous.

'Don't you think this could be the cause of your anorexia?' the male psychologist asked suddenly.

The question took me by surprise. I was used to sympathy and people going out of their way to make me feel comfortable, not interrogation. The cause of my anorexia had never been discussed before, and I hadn't prepared an answer.

'I don't know,' I stuttered. I felt defenceless and confused by their aggressive attitude. I feared that, if I didn't give them the answers that they wanted to hear, I would go away without the money I so desperately needed.

After more questions, which I didn't know how to answer, I was dismissed and walked out of the room feeling shaken. Mum and Dad were waiting outside, and, trying not to cry, I said, 'Let's just go.'

My parents wanted to know what the psychologists had said that had upset me so much, and I told them that they had suggested that our lifestyle was making me ill. Mum scoffed at this and said they didn't know what they were talking about. But perhaps my silence and confusion had given the professionals all the information they needed to know, because I got the funding.

I settled into the routine of the clinic fairly easily. My meals were planned and cooked for me and all I had to do was eat them. After a couple of days of having to feed me, the staff nipped the situation in the bud, saying I had to put the food in my mouth myself. I did everything that was asked of me and paid the price with the torment in my head. Fortunately, Diane was there to help me sort that out.

After our initial meeting I saw her once a week for therapy sessions. It soon became apparent that I needed more and she arranged for us to get together twice a week. Once I started to talk about my life I couldn't stop. My words tumbled over each other, like a torrent of water. With the words came fury, which bubbled through my system, and I was scared that, if I didn't keep talking, it would consume me.

I didn't know what the anger was about at first, so I simply let it pour out. I made a lot of noise and released years of pent-up grief and pain with screams and howls, while tears streamed down my cheeks.

Diane didn't let me hit myself, and I was grateful to her for showing me how to get my emotions out. We met in my bedroom and she would scatter large cushions around, and encouraged me to hit them when I felt angry. The trouble was, they were too soft and I needed to feel my punch meet with something solid, so I thumped the floor.

I wasn't allowed to go out for the first few months as I was weak and the risk of collapse was too great. I pottered around, attending various group sessions, and often went into the art room to play the piano or draw.

I kept a diary and wrote down every negative thought I had, and during the evening a carer would read it and reply to it with a positive affirmation. The whole place was about building confidence. Most people there were starting from scratch. The nature of the illness made each one of us believe that we were better than everyone else, but the truth was we were all self-loathing wrecks.

Not all the staff understood the fragile mindset of us anorexics, though. Sasha, the art teacher, was particularly adept at unwittingly putting her foot in it. 'Oh, hello, Lindsey, you're looking better,' she would cheerfully say as she busied herself, laying out paper and paints for the morning's session. She might just as well have said, 'Blimey, you're fattening up nicely, sumo girl!'

I liked most of the patients and got on especially well with two or three of them. Outside of mealtimes we were like a normal gang of teenagers, having a laugh, chatting and smoking. Bea taught me how to roll cigarettes and inhale properly, and she and I sat in the big garden puffing away together.

For most of my time there I shared a room with Gabby. My volatility in therapy sessions meant that no one in the building was left in any doubt about my anger and pain, and Gabby was sympathetic and supportive, partly because she really cared and partly, I suspect, because she wanted to avoid addressing her own problems.

After a while, I noticed that she wasn't talking to me so much, and I asked her why. She just buried her head in her arms and wouldn't say anything to me. I was worried that I had done something to upset her and racked my brains to think what it was. I found out later that her therapist had told her to stop spending so much time thinking about me and concentrate more of her energy on getting herself well.

Mum rang me every day to see how I was. I dreaded the phone calls, as I thought she might be able to tell that I had been discussing our secret life with strangers. I felt as if I were betraying my parents, but I also felt that I had no choice. I had to get to the bottom of why I didn't want to eat, because I wanted to live.

I stopped answering Mum's calls and tried to put my family to the back of my mind. If I get well, I thought, I'll have plenty of time to repair my relationship with Mum. I was being selfish but I knew my time at the clinic was precious and would soon be over.

Chapter Twenty-Five

Leaving Mum

After I refused to talk to Mum on the telephone she started sending me letters. I opened them with Diane, terrified of the power of the words on the pages. My mental state was fragile, and the slightest upset put my recovery back.

Mum didn't mince her words, and I got her message loud and clear. She said the Devil had caught me when I was mentally weak, and I was not to try to think for myself, but to let God into my heart to help me get well again. I desperately wanted to follow her words of advice, but the discoveries I was making during my sessions with Diane took me further and further away from the God that Mum talked about, the one I had grown up loving.

I didn't set out to abandon Mum and Dad's, and indeed my, beliefs, but it became obvious very soon after I started therapy that, in order to understand where my anger came from, I had to challenge the choices that my parents had made for me. The more I questioned what they had done, the more I realized how much our repressive and restrictive lifestyle had contributed to my mental illness. I really didn't want to believe it was true, but I couldn't deny the simple fact that I was getting better, and the only things that knocked my progress were letters from Mum.

My sessions with Diane were the key to my ongoing recovery at the clinic. Meal times were agonizing and it would often take more than an hour for me to eat a cereal bar, while I struggled to ignore the negative voice in my head that told me I was evil for eating. Eating was making me well, but getting better was taking me further away from my parents. Diane wrote quotes from the Bible on cards, which I placed on the dining table and read while I ate. The words gave me courage to put food in my mouth, and I felt I was doing what God wanted.

I sent a letter of my own to Mum, saying that I needed to explore the worldly world a little. I said that I wanted to wear trousers and go to the cinema, and do the things that normal teenagers did. I felt that if I experienced these things I would be able to make an informed choice about my future. I trusted that God would help me know what to do, but I underestimated how threatened Mum would feel about it.

Her agitated responses about Satan having taken over my soul confused me. Why was she so scared of the Devil, when she believed unwaveringly that God would win the war over evil? It made me feel uncertain about the belief system Mum and Dad devoted their lives to.

I went ahead and bought my first pair of trousers when I was allowed to take trips into the city. I chose a pair of black corduroys, identical to some Gabby had. In Top Shop the feeling of excitement and freedom that I had felt on the bus journey vanished beneath a familiar feeling of embarrass-ment and awkwardness. I felt so out of place among all the trendy worldly girls, but I knew I had to push myself to overcome my fears. Back at the clinic, I showed off my new purchase and everyone said they looked wonderful, but I felt like a stranger in my own skin.

I recognized that my discomfort was not because I was doing something wrong in the eyes of God, but due to years of believing I was different from other girls. With despair, I realized that this feeling was not going to be shaken off easily, no matter how many times I wore my new trousers.

My solution was to tell Mum and Dad that I wouldn't be going home when I left the clinic. I knew then that, if I returned to the suffocating lifestyle that we lead, I would certainly become seriously ill again, and probably die.

I made a rare telephone call to Mum and asked her if she and Dad could come and visit me the following Saturday, as I had something important that I wanted to tell them. I waited for them to arrive with my heart in my mouth. I felt so scared and vulnerable, as I was aware that the sight of them might cause me to weaken in my resolve.

I accepted Mum's hug stiffly when she put her arms around me. 'What's the matter, Lindsey?' she asked. I had never felt so unlike myself when I gave them my news. I listened to my own voice saying the words that I had practised over and over again with Diane, and I couldn't quite believe that I was speaking them.

'Mum, I'm not coming home. I can't go back to the Fellowship, it will kill me.'

Mum let out a strangled scream and tried to block the door, when, frightened, I made an attempt to leave the room. Dad calmed her down, and I stood looking at them both.

Much as I felt I didn't know myself, I also found it hard to see the parents I had left behind just six months ago in the two people who stood before me. In her headscarf and

Fellowship garb, Mum looked the same, and Dad wore his usual grey trousers and sandals as he always had, and I assumed that the distance I felt was because I had changed so much. I wasn't a Fellowship girl any more, but I felt far from being a worldly one.

I cut my hair off shortly after that, making my first visit to a hairdresser. I went to one recommended to me by Christine, another patient who had become a good friend. The hairdresser asked me if I was sure I wanted to cut off my long hair. Without a second's hesitation I replied yes, and she set to work. She carefully snipped off my hair, plaited the offcuts, and handed the plait to me. I didn't feel anything but excitement and eagerness to see what I looked like with short hair. I was mildly disappointed to find I didn't feel very different, apart from having a cold neck. I had asked staff and patients to sponsor my haircut, and gave the money to charity.

My good childhood friend Natalie wrote and visited me often. We had kept in contact over the years, with the occasional telephone call. She had been shocked to discover that I was so desperately ill and, in true Natalie style, made sure I knew that she cared about me.

Her then boyfriend, Alex, was a body piercer and I got it into my head that I wanted a stud in my nose. Natalie said that Alex would do it, and a couple of weeks later they drove up to Norwich. Alex stayed in the car, which he parked out of sight of the clinic, while Natalie came to request if she could take me out. The staff agreed and, giggling, we ran around the corner to where the car was pulled onto the kerb of a quiet road.

I hadn't met her boyfriend before, but, after a quick hello, he got to work. Alex instructed me to sit in the front seat, and Natalie sat in the other. She held my hand while he sat in the back, reached through and secured me with his left arm across my chest. Before I knew it he was stapling a hole in my nose with a large, indiscreet stud. Despite the bulbous swelling that was developing beneath the enormous jewel I'd never felt so cool in my life.

My time at the clinic was coming to an end and I needed to make a decision about whether I would apply for more funding to lengthen my stay to nine months. I made the choice easily. I felt that it was all very well making brave decisions while I was cushioned by the love of the staff at the clinic, whose job it was to make me feel good, but the real test would be if I could stand by those decisions in the outside world. I had to leave, and find out, and nothing was going to stop me.

Some of the staff were doubtful about my plans to go so soon. I think it must have suddenly dawned on them that under their care I had transformed from a severely underweight girl and devout Christian into a slim, apparently confident woman, who had rejected her parents' faith. The manager suggested that I should find a church to attend. I wasn't against the idea because I certainly hadn't abandoned God, just Mum and Dad's idea of Him.

I was told about a Christian man called Robert Lewellyn, who was in his nineties, but respected for his kindness and wise words. I wasn't sure what I wanted, and was ready to explore all of my options, so I decided to give him a visit.

I had afternoon tea with him. He was a tall, white-haired gentleman. When we said goodbye he pushed a rosary into my hand, saying a woman had given it to him and she trusted him to know whom to pass it on to. I took it to mean that he thought I was special in some way, but I rather suspect that, having heard my story, he thought I needed all the help I could get.

He also informed me that a former Open Fellowship member was now a priest of a large church in Norwich. I thought there wasn't any harm in seeing what he had to say, so I paid him a visit too. He didn't say much, and the words he did say weren't of much help. 'I'm sure your parents did their best,' he said, desperately looking around the room as if seeking some words of wisdom to give me.

Against the wishes of all the staff except Diane, I prepared to leave. One morning I told everyone that I was going into the city, and I would be back in the afternoon. I didn't say where I was going, as I didn't want anyone to stop me. First, I bought myself a street map of Norwich, then dropped into the Citizens' Advice Bureau, as suggested by Diane, and picked up a list of reputable letting agencies. I chose one at random, which went by the name Mitchells. I located their premises on the map and paid them a visit.

'Hi, I'm looking for somewhere to live,' I said after I had been shown into the boss's office. 'I've never rented anywhere before so please don't mess me around! I'll be receiving housing benefit because I have a mental health problem,' I added quickly, 'so there won't be any trouble with paying the rent.'

The man behind the desk looked a bit taken aback, but quickly recovered and said, 'Of course. I have just the thing. Come back this afternoon and I'll drive you over to see it.'

I spent the next few hours wandering around the city, poking around little bookshops, and constantly checking the clock on the tower of City Hall. I willed the hours to go by, then strolled slowly back to Mitchells.

I don't know quite what I was expecting, but it certainly wasn't the tiny bedsit that I was shown. It had a sink in one alcove and room for a bed about two paces across the room from the basin. There were a table and chair for one person, and a rail to hang my clothes on.

'I'll take it,' I said immediately.

The terraced house on Magdalen Street was smoky, and stank of dope, and the shared bathroom was grotty, but it was heaven to me.

The man from Mitchells drove me back across the city and dropped me off at the clinic. I strode into the house to be met by cross faces and severe words. 'Where have you been, Lindsey?' the staff asked. 'We've been worried about you.'

'I've found somewhere to live,' I announced.

And that was it. My time at Newmarket House was over, and, for the first time, I was about to set up home on my own.

'You'll need a TV,' one of the carers said as I left. 'I've managed all these years without one,' I answered cheerfully. 'I'll manage for a while longer.'

Victor helped me move my stuff, and Gabby's mum kindly equipped me with a stereo and bike. In the evening, when Victor had driven back to London, I sat alone in my new little home. I was aware of the huge responsibility I had to keep myself well, and, with this in mind, I set about making myself some tea.

Chapter Twenty-Six

Naming My Change

I didn't have any contact with my parents and Samantha after I left the clinic and, against Victor's wishes, I actively discouraged them from contacting me. Victor had no intention of returning to the Fellowship himself, but was worried about how I might cope without it. I wasn't trying to be nasty by refusing contact, but rather preparing myself for the inevitable rejection that would come when they returned to the Fellowship.

Victor told me that I was hurting Mum's feelings and that my parents couldn't understand why I was doing what I was. I could hardly understand it either, but I knew I had to carve out a life for myself, and seeing Mum and Dad just made that more difficult.

I don't do things by halves, and to make myself feel more complete as an individual, and less part of my family or the Fellowship, I changed my name by deed poll. I wasn't trying to alter my whole identity, so I simply dropped my surname and took my middle name as my last.

The first letter I received from Mum with 'Miss L Rosa' written on the envelope made me weep. It made me feel so guilty, as though I had pushed my parents into a corner and made them bow to my wishes. In my confusion I swung between thinking on the one hand how much they loved me and how undeserving I was of that love, and on the other hand questioning why (and this was the thing that upset me most), if they loved me so much, *why* did they watch me suffer without getting help sooner?

I put these questions to Diane, whom I still saw for regular therapy sessions. She never gave me the answers, as that wasn't her style of counselling, but she supported me in the decisions I made, and for this I shall be ever grateful. She was the only person in my life who understood how vital it was for me to take the reins of my life, which had always been controlled by Fellowship values.

At her suggestion I attended group therapy sessions that supported anyone who felt they needed it, not just people like me who had an eating disorder. This was an important step for me, as it made me realize that I wasn't unique in having a complicated life. It also meant that I began to widen my social circle in Norwich. I knew that friends were a significant part of my ability to survive without my family, and I tried to meet as many people as I could.

I got myself involved in voluntary work at a charity shop. This proved to be a great way to expand my sparse wardrobe, and furnish my bedsit. I had first choice of the stuff that was donated to the shop and picked out short skirts and dresses, and sleeveless tops. I wore these clothes with confidence, and I thought I looked great in them now that I was slim.

I firmly believed that the key to my being accepted in the world was my physical appearance. However, without the constant monitoring of the staff at the clinic, it wasn't long before I became locked into rigid eating patterns again. Actually, this was not driven by my desire to lose weight, because at seven and a half stone I thought I looked fine, but rather by my fear of putting weight on. This thought preoccupied my mind constantly, and I lived my life around it, preferring to eat at home on my own, where I could control my intake, rather than eat out with my new friends.

Christine took me under her wing when she too was discharged from the clinic. We visited her parents' farm in Norfolk, and we spent lazy days at her grandmother's converted barn on the north coast.

It was strange, the two of us attempting to convince ourselves and each other that we were over our eating disorders. At the clinic we had been open about our problems, and supported our friends, but outside of that environment it felt absolutely crucial that we keep our struggles secret. I recall feeling that I believed I would be judged for not managing to keep my mental illness at bay. I had so much to prove and couldn't stand failure.

On one of our trips we stopped at a grocery store to buy provisions for our stay at the barn.

'What do you want, then?' Christine asked casually. I considered my answer carefully. I didn't want to pick anything low-fat, as that would alert her to the fact I wasn't eating properly, but I didn't want to choose anything that might make her think I was greedy.

'A pizza?' I suggested cautiously. 'It'll be easy to cook,' I added quickly in case she thought I was being too gluttonous.

It was the same in the pub, both of us sipping our calorie-laden drinks, checking how much each other had drunk from the corners of our eyes. Our failure to have a good time, and our ability to deny that we were miserable, was spectacular.

I continued to go to the hairdresser and gradually my hair got shorter until I was a skinhead. I felt strangely sexy, despite my extreme androgynous look. I fancied men, but didn't make an effort to make any moves on them. For a start, I didn't know how to and, second, the feeling that I wasn't part of their world and acceptable to them never left me for a moment. However, my confidence was boosted by the interest shown in me by a handful of blokes, who, unfortunately, always happened to be the ones I didn't like.

I was keen to broaden my knowledge of the wider world and listened to Radio 4 whenever I could. Much of what I learned appalled me. The suffering of children worldwide especially tugged at my heart strings, my own difficult childhood leading me to have a particular interest in kids. I picked up a *Big Issue* one day, and found an advertisement for a sponsored event, dedicated to helping get homeless children off the streets. The event was a solo parachute jump, and I quite literally leapt at the chance to do something useful.

The training for the jump was to take place in the middle of the Fens, and I once again called on the services of Natalie, who, with boyfriend in tow, came to my rescue. She ferried me back and forth for two days between the hotel where we stayed and the airfield, where the big event was to occur.

After I jumped, or I should say was pushed, out of a small aeroplane, I suddenly realized I couldn't remember any of the instructions that I had been given. I looked towards the ground and to my horror couldn't see the airfield. We had been shown where to land, and it was obvious that I was nowhere near it. As the ground raced up to meet me the only words of the instructor I could recall were, 'Keep your feet together when you land, otherwise you'll break your legs.'

I kept my feet together all right, and rolled as I had been taught, landing on my back. My relief quickly turned to terror as the parachute filled with air and started tugging at me. There was an upper weight limit for people attempting the jump, but not a lower one as far as I knew, but I really wished there had been. I lacked the strength in my skinny body to get the parachute under control, but I didn't give up without a fight. The trouble was, that was what it looked as if I'd been doing when I got back to the airfield: having a fight. I'd trudged back, passing through two enormous fields, which, unfortunately for me, had just been ploughed, leaving peaks and troughs that felt like mountains to climb. While everyone else returned with their parachutes folded neatly in their arms, I stumbled in with mine trailing behind. I dumped it and made a quick exit before the instructor told me to tidy it up and checked for holes in the expensive equipment.

How stupid! I thought to myself as I left. You get in a plane for the first time in your life, and then you jump out.

That was one worldly experience I was more than happy never to repeat.

I started volunteering as a youth worker, taking kids who found mainstream school difficult to do archery and sailing. The thought that I might discover a grand solution for every child with problems persisted, and spending time with these teenagers made me even more determined to find a philosophy for the ideal childhood.

I consulted Diane about my concerns and she told me that her sister, Catherine, worked as a helper at a Steiner mother-and-toddler group. I knew nothing about Rudolf Steiner, the German spiritual philosopher who developed a set of rules for the upbringing of children, and so did some research. I really liked what I found out and arranged to meet with Rupert, who ran the sessions.

He was a funny chap, nervy and edgy, and not at all interested in my background, which suited me just fine. I had a habit of telling everybody I met about my life. I felt that it was inevitable that they would find me weird, so wanted to immediately give the reason why I was. In retrospect, I cringe, because it was undoubtedly *more* weird to give my life story to every stranger that I met. Rupert didn't seem to notice my weirdness, or just didn't care, and it was arranged that I'd start helping him out at the mother-and-toddler sessions.

Chapter Twenty-Seven

The Truce

A year or so after I left the clinic, my parents and I called a truce. Nothing was said, but both parties understood that if we were to have any kind of relationship we would have to avoid talking about the things that highlighted the differences between us, namely religion and the right way to live life. I was more than happy to comply. I had a romantic notion that, if I showed them that the way I was living was not ruining me, they might also be won over by this 'worldly' life. My dream, of course, was that they would give up on their mission of returning to the Fellowship and join me in the world.

I tentatively made contact with them, first by letter, in which I expressed my desire for a reunion. I can only guess at my parents' reaction, but my overriding impression was that they were delighted to have contact with me again.

I admired their willingness to look past all of the obviously more worldly aspects of my life. I now wore trousers and a nose ring, and had my hair cut into a skinhead style. I smoked rollups and carried a mobile phone. Landlines were not a problem for them, but they thought that mobiles were a direct link to the Prince of Darkness. As for the hair, well simply not wearing a token or headscarf was bad enough. Still, they managed to come to terms with all of that (probably blaming the Devil for influencing me), and I finally began to let myself believe that maybe, just maybe, I was more important to them than the Fellowship.

We agreed to meet. I set the boundaries. I was not ready for them to come to my home, as this was the only place I felt safe and I didn't as yet trust my parents not bring their madness into my personal space. I knew that I wouldn't be able to cope with the force of their misguided love and that I would be overpowered by my love for them. If this happened I could not trust myself not to simply hold up my hands and say, 'Take me home, it's all been a terrible mistake.' I love my mum and dad so much. So I created deliberate boundaries that not only stopped them trying to take me back to their home, but stopped me taking myself.

Our first meeting was on neutral territory. They drove to Norwich and picked me up from outside my bedsit on Magdalen Street. I had not been so close to Samantha and Mum and Dad for a long time. God, I almost felt drunk with the desire to be with them again. But I stood fast. We decided to go to Spalding, where there was a huge flower festival going on. During the long car journey I chatted with Mum and Dad about everything that was going on in my life. I deliberately mentioned the things that I knew would offend them. I had to test the strength of their conviction to take me as I was now. I talked of my work in the Steiner nursery, and my trips to the cinema. I told them of my charity work, and how I did a parachute jump to raise money for homeless children. I laid myself bare for them to see and waited for the backlash. But none came.

Samantha stayed pretty quiet, grinning at me occasionally. I could tell she was pleased to see me, and, although we didn't have much to say to each other, just being close to her again made me feel warm inside.

The day went without a hitch. We walked together, talked together and ate together. The only thing that marred it for me was the obvious difference in the way we looked. Samantha and Mum wore their Fellowship attire – their headscarves and long skirts – and I strutted around in my jeans and baggy jumper.

I felt the familiar embarrassment ride over me again. I was so desperate to be acknowledged by the world, and here I was undermining that by hanging around with the weirdos. As with so many other negative feelings I had, though, I pushed them down and tried to forget about them.

This meeting gave me confidence. Soon I was chatting to Mum regularly on the telephone, letting her back into my daily life. I felt in control, as if I was holding my parents to ransom. If they challenged me about my lifestyle I could stop contact again. I knew they did not want to take this risk.

We arranged for me to visit. The first time I went home was strange. The last time I had been there I was a six-stone waif, physically on my last legs. Mum had been feeding me like a small child and I went with her everywhere. Now I was returning as a twenty-year-old adult. I felt a million miles away from the pathetically needy girl I had been then. Even the house seemed different, as if it had shrunk. I felt like an oversized doll in a doll's house.

I smoked my cigarettes in my bedroom, blowing the smoke out through the window, and hung my trousers in my old wardrobe. I did not close my eyes when Dad thanked the Lord for our food. I used my mobile phone to ring my friends.

When I left I felt as if I had won a battle, but the war was not over yet. They still very obviously lived like Fellowship members and I wondered how I'd persuade them to live otherwise.

Chapter Twenty-Eight

Another New Life

I packed the last of my things into the car and drove across town to my lovely flat overlooking the city. Ten years had passed since I moved from the clinic into my little bedsit on Magdalen Street, and so much had changed in that time. And yet I felt the same kind of freedom I'd felt then. I was starting a new life, leaving the past behind me. Freedom was what I was after.

This may seem incredible, because I was leaving behind two children: Nina, who was four, and Stanley, who was still only one. But it wasn't from them that I was glad to be getting away. It was from my partner of nine years, the person who had seen me change from a naïve twenty-year-old with barely any experience of adult life to the fully formed person I'd become. I felt that there was no more work to do. I was the complete item, at last. I didn't need him, I didn't want him and I didn't love him. He was holding me back, just as the Fellowship had when I was a child.

Moving on had worked for me before, and it would work for me again. I was sure about what I had to do. Absolutely certain.

I told myself that the children would be fine with their dad, they would still see me almost every day, and I would be a better mum if I could find happiness. And I knew that happiness was just around the corner. I couldn't wait to get on with it. Going out, dressing up, and acting like a woman – all the things I'd missed out on when all I was thinking about was starving myself.

At the flat I looked out of my window past the ruined Norman tower that was once part of the old city wall, past the football ground, and over towards Thorpe on the opposite bank of the river. Living in my little bedsit on Magdalen Street, I never imagined I'd end up in this situation. How could I?

It had all started with a chance meeting, a twist of fate, which changed my life forever.

Tina was one of the first friends I made outside the clinic and, through her, I was able to start experiencing a social life of my own. She was a fun person with no inhibitions, who could just walk straight up to a stranger in a pub and start a conversation. I looked to her as an example of how to behave in the world.

She took me on camping trips, to music festivals and, when she decided to move into a house in the city, asked me if I wanted to rent the front bedroom from her. It was an offer I couldn't refuse; a chance to live a worldly life with friends, not as a patient at a clinic, or on my own in a bedsit.

I was still living at my bedsit when Tina celebrated her birthday. I walked across town to her house, buying a bunch of flowers on the way, intending to get there early as we'd agreed. Arriving at her door, I rapped confidently to make sure she would hear from the kitchen or back garden. Then I waited. It took a while before I saw her through the patterned glass, coming downstairs and across the room, with very little on. She was usually an early riser, the outdoor type, so I was surprised she wasn't dressed.

A tired-looking Tina opened the door, wearing just a T-shirt, which didn't actually cover anything down below. I strode straight in impatiently, feeling a bit put out that she wasn't ready to seize the day.

Tina's terrace had been modified so that it was completely open-plan downstairs. Originally there would have been two rooms separated by a stairway and cupboard, but now it was one huge room, with the stairs moved over to one side. On this occasion a large double camp bed was set up just inside the doorway to my right. I could hardly miss it as I walked in, and was horrified to see two bodies peering out from under a large white duvet.

Of course, I wanted to dash out again immediately, but I was already standing several feet inside the door, and Tina was closing it behind me, clutching her flowers. Instead of saying anything, I did what I always did in embarrassing situations, which was to make out that I wasn't bothered. I plonked myself down on the floor by the wall, crossed my legs and waited, trying to ignore what was right in front of me. Why I didn't just head straight through to the kitchen under the pretence of needing to put the flowers into a vase of water, I don't know. All I could do was stare forward blankly at the two bodies, which were now looking rather uneasy.

One of them, the blonde, was Tina's friend Rachel, whom I'd met on a couple of occasions. The other turned out to be a dark-haired man, whom I'd never seen before. It soon became apparent that Tina had someone upstairs with her. I was really upset. It was supposed to be *our* day.

I found trusting people really hard. I could cope with one-to-one relationships with friends, but I didn't know how to act with groups of people, and needed to prepare myself for situations like that. Silently I blamed Tina for not warning me.

Eventually, Tina reappeared, followed by another dark-haired man I later learned was Martin. By this time, the chap in the camp bed had sat up, apparently trying to reach for his clothes without exposing his nakedness. Tina offered to give him and Martin a lift home, and, before I knew it, we were all crammed into her car heading in that direction.

I sat in silence on the back seat near the window. In the middle next to me was the camp-bed man. He looked serious and moody and didn't say much. He just stared forward, steadying himself with an outstretched arm, holding onto the side of the driver's seat.

His apparent arrogance unsettled me, but I could not help liking his strong-looking arm. His shirtsleeve was rolled up, and it was right there in front of me. I tried to ignore it.

At Martin's place there were two more men. My uneasiness grew. They had driven over from Cambridge with the camp-bed man for a night out. All four had headed to Boswell's nightclub in the Tomb Land area of Norwich, for an evening of drinking. Tina and Martin had got talking and Camp-Bed Man ended up with Rachel.

We left them there and headed back to Tina's house to get ready for the garden party she was having in the afternoon. Sitting in the living room on the cushions Tina preferred to chairs, we smoked some rollups and the conversation turned to the events of the previous night. Tina was talking about how much she liked Martin, wondering if he liked her and speculating on what exciting things might come of it.

'I like Tom,' I said.

Tina and Rachel sniggered. I knew what they were thinking. 'Silly little Lindsey, who knows nothing about boys. Now she has a childish crush on the camp-bed man. How sweet.' They were in their mid-thirties, I was just twenty.

The funny thing was that, just the day before, the thought had popped into my head that I didn't need a boyfriend. I'd recently had a date with a man called Ian, who said he was in love with me. He didn't really know anything about me, but seemed to think that I was some sort of angel. He wrote me love letters and gave me books about Mother Teresa.

After the Ian experience, I had decided to forget about trying to meet someone. Part of me felt removed from sexuality because of my anorexic state, and another part still held the belief that I couldn't have a boyfriend, anyway, as I was a Fellowship girl. I was asexual, just a being hanging between two worlds.

Martin turned up at Tina's party in the afternoon and they began a relationship, which lasted a couple of months. This was a bit of a blow, as I'd been really looking forward to spending time with Tina when I moved in. It was clear that now she would be spending all her time with him.

The weekend after the party was a bank holiday and a series of social events were planned involving Tina, Rachel and me, plus Martin, his friends and brothers. Tom was also heading over from Cambridge.

What I didn't know was that Tina had told Martin about my crush on Tom, and he, in turn, had told Tom. It was just as well I didn't know he had been told – I would have died of embarrassment.

On the Friday, there was a lot of flirting going on between Tom and Rachel. I buried my head in a book I'd grabbed from Martin's book shelf so that no one would try to talk to me, all the time wishing I could be as confident as the other worldly girls. I was secretly glad the next day when Rachel had to head home to finish some work.

From then on, Tom and I started to get to know each other. Martin's brothers and a couple of their friends turned up, having driven down from Salford, and we all decided to go on one of the tourist river trips along the Wensum. I was standing at the dock, looking defiant, wearing my frayed checked trousers and tie-dye T-shirt. My hair was short and red, gelled into spikes. To make myself feel, and look, a bit more feminine I put on an Alice band. I stared at Tom, much as I had done when I'd been sitting in Tina's living room the week before. He later told me that it was that defiant stance that interested him.

We sat together on the boat trip, laughing at the tour guide's comments, which seemed to declare that every object we saw was the oldest building in the city. Tom seemed really attentive. Later on, too, when we were in a pub near Martin's house, playing pool and watching a bit of football on the television above the bar. We laughed about the commentary, trying to recall as many bad pundit clichés as we could think of.

'It's a game of two halves. They need to score if they're going to win. The lads are giving a hundred and ten percent.'

That evening we all headed to Boswell's, inevitably. I'd stayed at Tina's the previous night and didn't have a change of clothes, so she lent me a chiffon blouse. 'Doesn't she look beautiful?' Tina said to Tom on the way out of Martin's house. He nodded, trying not to show his distaste for the oversize top.

I'd drunk so much the night before that I didn't feel like having any alcohol. Besides, I didn't want to lose control in front of Tom and look a fool. Tom wasn't showing so much restraint and was drinking Guinness after Guinness. He started leaning over and putting his arm around me. I kept shrugging it off. It was ridiculous. All I wanted to do was snuggle into him but I just couldn't let myself go.

'Do you listen to music?' he slurred. I hadn't heard a lot at that point in my life. Only really what my friends Bea and Gabby had copied for me when I was at the clinic. It was a strange mix of each person's tastes.

'Yeah, ABBA, Robbie Williams, Garbage, Placebo, the Carpenters, Dusty Springfield,' I said.

He thought for a second. 'ABBA are good.'

Late in the evening, we ended up back at Martin's house. We all sat round listening to music while the drinking continued. Then, in the early hours, everyone decided that it was time to get some sleep. There were no beds for the visitors, but I'd made it clear that I was having the bit of floor by the wall in the front room. I laid out some cushions and found a throw to use as a blanket. That evening I'd already imagined a scenario in which Tom would join me, but I told no one about it.

'I'll sleep next to you, if you don't mind,' Tom suddenly said, and did so before I had a chance to really think too much about it. This was exactly what I'd fantasized about, and now it was happening. He put his arm around me and we lay there in the dark. Then, he kissed me. It was the first time I'd ever been kissed. I was twenty years old and didn't know what to do.

What do I do with my tongue, where do I put my teeth? I thought. In a moment he'll realize what a bad kisser I am and will push me away. He'll be disgusted with me.

I thought every worldly girl my age would know exactly how to kiss, having done it a thousand times.

I kept my knees clenched tightly together, even though I was still fully dressed. I could barely cope with the kissing, so I wasn't going to have his hand stray down there. It didn't.

The next day it was a sunny morning and everyone was up. My lips had a tingling sensation I'd never experienced before. Tom was smiling in my direction, but I couldn't look at him.

The weekend was drawing to a close, and Tom was planning to drive back to Cambridge that afternoon to get some rest before going back to work the next day. First, though, we walked to the Ferry Boat pub near the river, where we could buy a roast dinner and listen to live music. Tom sat next to me, but I still hadn't really looked at or spoken to him that morning.

Much as I was besotted with Tom, it was all far too much for me to cope with. I had to save him from me and tell him that I was fucked up and a bag-load of trouble. I was physically shaking, overcome with emotions I'd never felt before. Nothing in life had prepared me for this and I wasn't enjoying the feeling one bit. But I still couldn't help the fantasies raging in my head. The possibilities, the maybes.

'I need to speak to you, please, in private,' I said, after we'd eaten.

'Oh, right,' he said, sounding a little worried. 'Let's go outside.'

We sat down next to each other on a low wall.

'OK,' he said, inviting me to say whatever it was.

'There's something you should know. I'm not like everybody else. I was brought up in a very strict religion. I've left that,' I added hurriedly, 'but I'm anorexic and really fucked up. And I've never had a boyfriend before.'

Tom paused for a moment, thinking. Then, after a moment, he said, 'That's OK.'

He offered me his phone number, I took it, and we went back inside. I was gobsmacked at his stupidity. I'd given him a way out of the situation and he wasn't taking it. What the hell was going on?

I didn't know what I should do next, but I was filled with a feeling of excitement and happiness. A man had given me his phone number, and he wasn't Ian! I moved into Tina's house that week, recreating the ambience I'd created in my bedsit, but adding some wooden shelves I'd bought from Argos.

I thought hard about what to do next. I had to behave as a worldly girl would. It seemed to me she would be acting cool and not calling straightaway. I resisted for over a week.

I borrowed Tina's phone, pulling the cable out across the landing into my room so I had a bit of privacy. I wasn't really thinking about what Tom might be doing. He'd given me his number, so I assumed he wanted me to call.

At that time, Tom was back living with his parents, bedding down on the floor of their front room in a sleeping bag while their house extension was being knocked through. It was his dad who picked up the phone.

'Is Tom there?' I asked.

'Yes, I'll get him for you,' he said, forgetting to find out who was calling.

Then I heard Tom's voice. 'Hello?'

'Hi, it's Lindsey,' I said.

'Who?' came the reply.

My little bubble was instantly pricked. I had only been thinking about what I might say. It suddenly dawned on me that he was a person with thoughts and feelings and might not want to speak to me. Vulnerable was how I felt. A stream of thoughts rushed though my mind in an instant: How on earth had I thought that a worldly boy would want to talk to me? Nothing had changed. I was still a Fellowship girl after all this time.

'Lindsey,' I repeated.

'Oh, right! I couldn't hear what you said. My dad was just shutting the door. How are you?'

I felt so relieved.

Soon after that, Tom drove up to see me. To see *me*! Not Martin, although in those early days he did stay there a few times instead of at mine. He would drive up on the Friday after work, or sometimes on Saturday morning, stay Sunday night, then brave the early-morning traffic to get to work first thing Monday.

When he did start to stay with me, it put a strain on my friendship with Tina. I had become very good at appearing to be perfectly in control on the outside, so Tina began to rely on my words of wisdom to help with all of her obsessions and anxieties, unaware that my mental battles raged on inside. It suited me, as I gained her acceptance and compliments, while my own eating habits went unnoticed. But it became really difficult when Tom visited, as my loyalties were split. I still didn't know what the rules were.

One weekend, it was his birthday and he made the trip over to see me. When he arrived, Tina was in crisis talks with me about her relationships and was so frantic that I couldn't break off the conversation. Tom let himself in, tripping over the curtain rail that was laid out ready to be put up, and stood in the doorway waiting for some kind of welcome. It didn't come. Tina looked up for a moment, then carried on talking, and I just didn't know what to do.

'It's Tom's birthday,' I said at last.

'Oh,' she said, not really taking it in, and carried on talking.

Tom stood across the room, waiting.

I felt like I had to make a choice between my friendship with Tina and the man in my life who I was falling in love with. Tina had introduced me to so much, but Tom was different. I didn't feel like an ex-Fellowship or anorexic girl with him, I felt like Lindsey. The choice was simple.

The one thing I wasn't ready for was sex. I'd only just kissed for the first time and still had crippling body issues. I was throwing up after every meal, and had an iron grip on my eating habits. Soon after I met Tom, the reality that I had a boyfriend began to sink in, and I lost myself again. There was nothing else I could do. It was all far, far too real. If there was one thing I was adept at doing, it was putting up a wall to protect myself from getting hurt.

Tom could see that I'd changed, but didn't really understand what was going on. Not then. The first thing that happened to me was a rapid loss of weight. I was about seven stone ten when we met, which was thin but healthy. I hadn't got my periods back, and wouldn't for a year or two still, but I looked pretty normal.

But, over the next six months or so, I went down and down until the needle on the scales no longer reached seven.

If I knew I was seeing Tom at the weekend, I'd spend all week preparing, knowing that there was a good chance we'd eat out and drink lots, and I wouldn't be able to keep a check on my intake. In front of him, I wanted to make sure I seemed as normal as possible.

Monday through to Friday, I'd eat nothing for breakfast, but had an apple at eleven a.m. For lunch I ate a jacket potato topped with low-fat cottage cheese. Dinner was pasta with sliced banana and ketchup. All I would drink was black coffee or water.

When Friday arrived and I was about to see Tom, I wouldn't eat or even drink anything all day, ensuring that my stomach was as flat as possible. It was a process of starving during the week, eating at the weekend, and it went on for most of the year.

My thinness gave me confidence. I had bought a short plaid dress from the charity shop I worked in, and wore this with a pair of high-heeled leather boots. It wasn't something I'd dare put on if I were bigger, but, to me, thin was sexy.

Tom didn't share my opinion, but somehow that didn't make any difference. It wouldn't have mattered if he'd told me a million times he liked curves, I didn't believe him. That was the irony of the situation. I was starving myself to please him, but nothing would have pleased him more than to have a healthy-looking Lindsey with curves.

Diane advised me not to have sex for at least six months after I started seeing Tom. She knew how far I had to go to become comfortable with my body, and that doing such a thing any sooner would be absolute madness. I waited a month.

For some reason, we were staying at Martin's house rather than mine, sleeping on the futon he'd laid out in his attic conversion.

All I knew about sex was what I'd read in books. I put this into practice, not in the context of a romantic scenario, but by directing Tom as though I were a drill instructor. I'd expected multiple orgasms to be forthcoming, but I just didn't realize I'd have to connect with the other person to get them. Being that intimate with another human being was far more than I could deal with, so I simply shut myself off from the reality of the situation. This state of mind wasn't conducive to good lovemaking, especially as I was so aware of my body. My body may have been there in the moment, but my mind didn't turn up.

I felt so uptight about it that I just couldn't enjoy sex. I started to wonder if it was a problem with him. I felt as if he was blaming me, saying that I needed to relax. We should have taken Diane's advice.

The physical side of things was always going to be difficult. I hated my body, so how could I enjoy exposing it to someone else, and risk looking like a fool?

Chapter Twenty-Nine

Day Tripping

Our first holiday was a bit of a road trip. It was the kind of thing I'd dreamt of doing. It was the freedom I'd fantasized about and I saw it as a chance to escape the rigid routine I'd built my life around. It protected me from the world I feared, but with Tom I dared to let it go. We didn't book anywhere to stay, just headed from the shared house Tom had moved to in Cambridge, past Birmingham to Shrewsbury. One night we stayed in a B&B in Ludlow. It was a great little guesthouse, right next to a pub. We ate there, played pool and fed the juke box with coins. With 'Oliver's Army' and 'Suspicious Minds' belting out from the speakers, we got pleasantly drunk, stumbling out at closing time to make the long journey across the gravel car park to the front door of the B&B. It was there that we found we were locked out and had to wake up the apologetic owner, who'd forgotten all about us.

In the morning we took a look at Ludlow Castle, before heading south via Iron Bridge to the Malvern Hills. Finding somewhere to stay there proved a little more tricky, but we eventually managed to get somewhere high up on the west side with views all the way across to Wales. For our evening meal, we drove back around the hill to the town, and found a beautiful hotel with a glasshouse full of exotic ferns and cheese plants in huge pots. We sat by the bay window, with views from the terrace out over the silhouette of the town. On the way back, along a winding road that cut through a narrow pass in the hill, we noticed a brightly lit pub called the Wyche Inn, which was only a mile or so from our B&B. It was a warm night, so we walked the tree-lined road from where we were staying, got drunk again, and staggered home.

It had been a wonderful taster of 'worldly' life, drinking, eating out, travelling with the boyfriend I never thought I'd have, and I wanted it to go on forever. But when Tom said goodbye and I returned to Norwich, my courage left me and I became a slave to my crippling eating habits once again.

It must have been quite a few months later that we went to Amsterdam, because it was absolutely freezing. This time Tom had booked us into a hotel he'd heard about from a friend. It had been featured in a German film called *Heimat* and was shaped like a slice of Edam. We flew from Stansted to Schiphol, then took a short train ride into the city. It took a while to find our hotel, following a small map that led us across countless small bridges and canals.

Most of our time there was spent wandering the streets looking for somewhere warm to sit. Neither of us had the boots we needed to keep the snow from soaking our feet. We hadn't realized that almost all of the museums and galleries would be closed in the winter season, so, once again, we did a lot of drinking.

The one gallery we did visit was the Van Gogh Museum. I hadn't had much access to art growing up. Mum and Dad weren't against it, but they preferred museums with artefacts and historical information. There were only about three paintings in my parents' house, two of which were grim and dark. There was a skilfully painted scene of waves tossing boats about in a storm on the wall opposite my parents' bed.

Another painting in the front room downstairs was a sickeningly serene print mounted on a white background and surrounded by a fake mahogany frame. The picture was of an idyllic scene, featuring a flock of sheep being herded along a lane. Van Gogh's work sat nicely between the two extremes I'd grown up with.

Of course, it didn't take us long to find a 'brown café' serving more than just alcohol. At the back was a little kiosk with a bleary-eyed man sitting inside. I volunteered to make a purchase and handed over the equivalent of three pounds to receive a massive bag of grass in return. Tom's eyes nearly popped out of their sockets.

We bought ourselves a drink and sat on stools at the little round table near the front window. I wished I'd picked the seat by the door. There was no need to be ungenerous with the stuff as we had so much, so Tom rolled two fat joints using the extra-large papers we'd bought. I took a couple of long draws on mine, turned white and felt as if I was going to die.

'Lindsey,' said Tom, 'are you OK? You're not going to be sick, are you? If you are, go to the toilet.'

I said nothing. My head was spinning so much, all I could do was shut my eyes and lay my face down on the table.

'I'm going to be sick,' I mumbled at last.

'Go to the toilet,' Tom insisted.

'I can't move,' I said, and then I felt it rising up from my stomach. Only a few hours earlier I'd eaten the best meal I'd ever had. It was green peppers stuffed with rice and some kind of delicious sauce. Now I was going to see it again, and so was Tom.

I grabbed a pint glass and filled the thing.

'Shit,' cursed Tom. 'Come on, let's go.'

I didn't move, there was more to come. Much more.

Seeing me convulse, Tom shoved the ashtray under my nose and I filled that to the top, too.

'Christ, we must look like a right pair of green tourists,' commented Tom.

There was nothing left to fill, but I wasn't done. I retched again, all over the tabletop.

Tom could do nothing but watch helplessly as the river flowed off the edge onto the floor.

Up to that point he had been hoping to sneak past the bar with the ashtray and pint glass and wash them out without the barman being any the wiser. To make this possible he'd shifted his chair round so that no one could see what was going on, but the game was up. He went up to the bar to ask for a mop. We didn't go back there again.

On one of the days we were there we tried wandering the streets to take in some of the sights, but ended up chilled to the bone. My shoe had a leak and my trousers were becoming soaked by the melting snow.

It got to the point where I was so cold that Tom became worried about me. I didn't have enough flesh on me to keep me warm. Back in our hotel room, he made the shower hot for me and pushed me in. As soon as I got out, he started piling towels and blankets on top of me. I was still shivering, so he lay on top of the entire pile. It was no good, I was still trembling violently. He ran downstairs to reception to ask for some boiled water to make a hot drink, but they told him they didn't have any facilities for that and he'd have to go across the road to a bar! It was a nice enough place, but the service was terrible.

Now that I felt sick at the sight of the grass, Tom was left to smoke it by himself.

'Just throw it away,' I suggested, but he wasn't going to be beaten.

'We're not wasting this,' he insisted.

Whenever he had the chance, he'd be leaning out of the window desperately trying to get through another joint, but, however much he put in it, there was still some left in the bag. I just wanted him to shut the damn window.

Pale-faced and stoned, Tom finally disposed of the remaining grass in an ashtray on the train back to the airport. I think it pained him to waste that last bit, but he'd done well to get that far.

Tom was very 'worldly', but he was also stable and reliable. The more time I spent with him, the further I moved from my Fellowship life of old, and the less it threatened me. Tentatively, I began speaking to Mum and Dad more often on the phone, and agreed to go on holiday to Jersey with them in the summer.

I had fond memories of our holidays together and a part of me hankered after those times when things had been easy. I flew from Norwich and met them in Jersey. I'd hardly ever flown before – the first time, I'd jumped straight out again with a parachute on my back. I felt like a real adult and was excited and filled with confidence. We stayed in a detached cottage on the coast. A beautiful spot. I shared a room with Samantha, just like old times. At night I listened to my music cassettes on my Walkman, the Rolling Stones' 'Sympathy for the Devil' and the Stranglers' 'Strange Little Girl' and their album *The Gospel According to the Meninblack*. Samantha sat on her bed and read the Bible.

We did our usual round of the tourist spots, visiting underground rooms where prisoners of war had been kept, and a number of museums. I watched Dad pore over the exhibits, leaning over to study them, with his hands clasped behind his back. I felt the same sense of boredom that I had when I was nine years old.

I struggled with the intensity of my reactions to our eating arrangements. At home I ate alone during the week, when Tom wasn't around. Despite my desire to be normal, since leaving the clinic I'd found it a continuous battle to stay healthy and well. The only way I managed was to eat my 'safe' foods. I figured that the main thing was to eat – I could tackle the unhealthy habits later on. There on Jersey I was under the scrutiny of Mum's sharp eyes. She piled my plate with food. Unsafe food. I felt overwhelmed by fear and horror as I finished every morsel. But I could not show my fear. I had to show them that I was well. I had to prove I had made the right decision.

One rainy afternoon we stayed at the cottage, reading and playing board games. Rather suddenly, Samantha said, 'Why don't we look at the weather forecast?' Dad reached for his newspaper, but she quickly said, 'No, I meant on the television.' I stayed absolutely still. The television had been covered with the usual tea towel as soon as we arrived, and was used as a little table for supporting the fruit bowl.

Then I said, 'You do know that everything's scheduled, don't you? I mean, you can't just turn the telly on and watch the weather forecast.'

'When is it on, then?' Samantha persisted.

This was so unlike her. She was usually so subdued and subservient, in a world of her own. I wondered if my being there was having the effect of making her start to ask questions about her lifestyle. Part of me felt delighted at her sudden interest in something worldly, but there was also a little niggle of fear. Samantha was so vulnerable. What if she did decide to leave home but couldn't cope with the extreme differences between the Fellowship way of life and the world beyond? I was finding it hard enough myself, almost unbearably so sometimes.

What happened next was so extraordinary I don't think I'll ever forget it.

It was agreed that I could turn on the television when I thought the news and weather forecast might be on. I checked the TV listings in Dad's newspaper and, at one thirty p.m., I found myself sitting in the living room on my own in front of the switched-on television. I was aware of Samantha hovering on the other side of the closed door.

I felt so odd. What was I doing? As soon as I had the information that we wanted I turned off the TV set. I did not feel good. In fact, I felt as if I had just brought the Devil into that tranquil holiday cottage.

After that, the television was covered up again and nothing more was said about it.

One evening I was sitting with Mum and Dad in the lounge. I was reading a novel by Jack Higgins and thoroughly enjoying it. Mum bustled around in the kitchen, doing the washing up. Dad was reading, too. He looked up suddenly and said, 'You know, Lindsey, you should read this.'

'What's that, Dad?' I said, hardly looking up from my own book.

'This.' He held up the book for me to see. I recognized the dark burgundy cover with gold embossed lettering, and a feeling of nausea came over me. But I concealed my feelings. This was a surprise. Just when I thought it was all going so well, Dad couldn't resist the temptation. I expect that, just like me, he needed to find out where I stood on the matters that meant so much to him. Well, he had certainly caught me off my guard this time.

'Come on, Dad, I don't think so. You know I don't believe all that stuff.'

I listened to Dad, backed occasionally by Mum, as he reiterated the values and beliefs of the Fellowship. It was as though someone had pressed a button, transforming them from relatively normal human beings into robots programmed by the Fellowship. This was a major shock for me.

Their conviction that the Fellowship was the right place to be was as strong as ever. This was fifteen years after being 'withdrawn from'. Sadly, it dawned on me that my dream was not going to be realized. Mum and Dad – and Samantha – were not going to be joining me in the world.

After that holiday I cooled things with Mum and Dad. That evening's events had shaken me more than I cared to admit.

But over the next few months, despite that potential hiccup in my plan to get my parents to leave their Fellowship ways behind, the desire to see them and be with them never left me. Gradually, the regular phone calls between me and Mum built up again, and I found myself feeling at ease with them. There was no mention of the Fellowship or God.

I decided to try another visit and it was arranged for me to stay with them.

That first evening we sat down for dinner, and we chatted animatedly. It was good to see them all again. It felt genuinely good to be back. Later on I lay down on the single bed that still occupied my old room. I felt relaxed. I wondered if I had been wrong to worry so much about coming home. Then Mum popped her head around the door and asked if she could come in. She entered and stood in front of me. I looked up at her smiling.

'What is it, Mum?' I asked.

'Lindsey, we have something to tell you,' she began.

She sounded pleased about whatever it was, but the smile left my face.

'This probably will be the last time we see you. The Fellowship have apologized to us and we're going back.' Her voice was calm, but I could see the happiness and light in her eyes.

The news hit me like a ton of bricks falling from a high building.

'No, no, *no!*' I howled. 'No, please no.'

She said, 'I'm sorry, Lindsey, but you know this is what we've been waiting for. We've never disguised the fact we wanted to go back. You have the choice to come with us.' She was so calm, while my emotions raged inside of me. I felt gutted, absolutely gutted. This wasn't supposed to happen. Please, please don't let this be happening, I thought.

'I'm so happy for you,' I said, forcing out the words. 'But you know I won't be doing that. I just can't believe what you believe. I just can't. It doesn't make sense to me. I don't even believe in God.'

I was shaking now. What was she asking me to do: leave Tom? No way. I buried my head in my pillow and, with that, Mum, her news bulletin over, left the room, closing the door behind her.

I suddenly felt terrified. What if they didn't let me leave the house? I had to get out of there immediately. Up until this point I had always trusted my parents, but now, for the first time, I didn't. Now I could see that we were different. I felt worldly and being in the house was completely wrong.

I found my mobile phone and rang Tom.

'Come and get me, now,' I demanded.

'What's happened?' he asked sleepily. It was nearly midnight. 'Can't it wait?'

'No, please come.' I explained the situation and he promised to come the next morning, claiming it was too late to hit the road at that time.

I spent a miserable, sleepless night in that house.

In the morning I ate nothing and spoke to no one. I stood by the window watching for Tom's car. He had never been here before and had never met my parents. I hoped he wouldn't get lost. At last his blue hatchback pulled up on the grass verge outside. I ran to the door and out onto the driveway. He grabbed me and took me in his arms. I clung to him, my head pressed against his chest. I really wanted just to go, and had my bags at the door ready.

'Come on, please,' I said.

Tom was hesitant. He hadn't even said hello to Mum and Dad, and I sensed he felt he ought to. He was saved the trouble of introducing himself, though, as Dad stepped forward.

'Would you like to come in?' I wasn't expecting this. I shook my head at Tom, who promptly said he would. Mum asked if he wanted to use the toilet, and then stood chatting to him in the kitchen. I kept quiet. I couldn't bring myself to look at Mum and Dad, let alone talk to them. I felt so betrayed.

After a few minutes Dad stepped into the room, clearing his throat. He'd been hanging around in the background waiting until the formalities were over.

'Ah, ahem, Tom, could you step in here a moment, please,' he said, gesturing towards the front room. I groaned inwardly. What the fuck was he going to say? Dad hated confrontations of any kind, so I was pretty sure it wouldn't be a full-blown dressing down.

Both men went into the room, and I followed, hanging back slightly. I observed the similarities between them. Both were tall and slim, one bald, the other balding, each obviously nervous and wary of the other.

'Ah, now, Tom.' He looked as if he was searching for the right words. 'You know that we are part of the Fellowship, which means we believe in the teachings of Christ.' He placed such emphasis on this last word that Tom almost laughed. 'It's nothing personal, but we can't have anything to do with you, as your lifestyle is not in keeping with ours.' I felt surprised. This wasn't a telling off, but rather an apology. My Dad was actually trying, albeit in a roundabout way, to say sorry that he could not have any kind of relationship with Tom because of the rules that he lived his life by. He might as well have said, 'No hard feelings then, eh, old pal?'

I could see that Tom was totally bemused, and I felt as though I should remove him from the madhouse that I had dragged him into.

My goodbyes were rather frosty, and masked my real emotion. In the car, however, I broke down and Tom drove as I held my head in my hands. I needed something to make me feel normal, to help me feel part of the real world again. I flicked through the radio stations, hoping to find comfort in familiar voices and music. I didn't find it. I felt lost and alone.

I had worked so hard to find my feet in this worldly world, while tolerating the Fellowship life my parents lead, and now I felt I had neither. Perhaps one part of me couldn't exist without the other, I thought. I wasn't ready to become a fully fledged worldly person, but now I had been shoved off the edge of the cliff. I had no choice now but to fly in the world. The decision had been made for me. So much for the real love the Fellowship believed existed only among themselves. Of course, a world run by the Devil could not have a place for real love. Now I could see for myself that not even the love between a mother and a daughter could compete with the might of the Fellowship.

Chapter Thirty

Becoming Worldly

I loved my trips to see Tom in Cambridge. After I'd finished my voluntary work, I'd head to the station and catch the Cambridge shuttle. Tom would pick me up straight from work and we'd head across the city to join in whatever social event was in progress at his house.

It was like walking into another world, compared with my existence in Norwich. At the clinic and at Tina's house, I'd got used to the company of other females, but this was a male household. They didn't care about how much they ate or drunk, and it was impossible to make a bigger mess than the one they had already created. I was made to feel welcome and no one cared about my past. On these weekends I gave myself permission to become the carefree girl I longed to be.

Tom was incredibly passionate about music, so, when we spent time in his room, he'd play me different albums that he thought I should listen to. One of the first things that grabbed me was a Creedence Clearwater Revival album. I loved the sound of it, but struggled to find the words to describe how it made me feel. It just felt sexy. Another time, he introduced me to Lou Reed's *Berlin*. I'd never heard anything with that kind of depth before. Unlike most albums, it took me on a journey.

One of Tom's housemates was a really funny guy called Ryan, who had been with him on that fateful trip to Boswell's. My ears pricked up when I learned that his brother's name was Kester. When I was a little girl, dreaming of a Fellowship marriage, I'd decided I was going to have seven children, two boys and five girls. One of the boys was to be called Aiden, the other Kester. I'd seen the name in one of my children's books and loved it.

The other housemate was Dave, who was obsessed with computer games and had two guinea pigs. Ryan's wardrobe didn't fit in his room and sat out on the landing, with Dave's guinea-pig hutch on top. Downstairs, Dave had a massive surround-sound system and TV, which he used continually to play the latest games. The table in front was usually a mass of overflowing ashtrays and bottles of alcohol, and, when Dave wasn't gunning down the enemy, the household would watch WWF wrestling.

One time Mum had been visiting me in Norwich and agreed to drop me off at Tom's on the way home. Halfway there, as it occurred to me, I suddenly said, 'Oh my goodness! I've forgotten my nightdress!'

There was a stony silence from Mum for a few seconds. 'You can borrow one of Tom's T-shirts, can't you?' she asked, but it was more of a statement than a question.

Tom was still at work when we arrived, but by this time things must have been going well because he'd given me a key.

'Come in, have a look round,' I said to Mum.

I still hadn't let go of the dream that one day Mum and Dad would abandon the idea of going back to the

Fellowship. I tried to include them in my new life whenever I could, forcing them to see who I was now. She reluctantly agreed to step inside the doorway but that was as far as she was prepared to go.

It was probably just as well, otherwise she'd have seen the TV and sound system in the living room, and huge posters of the wrestlers 'Stone Cold' Steve Austin, the Rock, Triple H and the Undertaker, Blu-Tacked to the kitchen cupboards.

'It smells smoky in here,' she commented, turning her nose up.

That evening there was a party at the house. I watched a bit of TV until Ryan arrived, followed by Dave, his girl-friend, Melissa, and a few others.

Tom rolled in later, very, very comfortably drunk. No else had come anywhere near drinking the amount he had.

'You're in fine form,' laughed Dave, but I felt embarrassed. Tom was lunging around, putting on CDs and being loud, while everyone else remained relatively quiet. I didn't want to stand out. At one point he winked at me, which was so out of character that he even said, 'What am I doing? I just winked at you!'

I just wanted the Tom I was used to. I had so little confidence in myself that I relied on his steadiness. I depended on him.

As the evening went on, Tom carried on drinking, but had become so used to the alcoholic effects that he seemed more sober. I was getting drunk along with everyone else and it inevitably ended in my being sick. I filled another pint glass, this time the one on the floor in Tom's room. He took me into the bathroom next door and sat with me, holding my forehead as I was sick in the toilet.

As we cuddled up back in the room, he said, 'I love you,' and then rolled over to go to sleep.

'No, you don't,' I said to the back of his head. I thought he was being foolish and couldn't wait for the morning when he'd be back to the Tom I knew.

Through a friend I managed to get a room in a very large family house in the Cathedral Close. The family who lived there took in a lot of the girls who had left the clinic and my friend, Christine, was living there in another room at the time.

One evening I passed Christine on the stairs. She looked directly at me, the way she does when she's decided to be very honest about something. 'Er, Lindsey,' she began. 'Er, why do you eat the same thing every day?' I could hardly breathe. 'What do you mean?' I replied, being careful not to let my voice reveal my dismay. 'I can smell your food when you cook it, and it's always the same.' I thought that her comments were a bit unfair, as I actually had three meals to my repertoire.

It was in the bedsit at Cathedral Close that I finally admitted to Tom that I was still very much in the grips of anorexia. It didn't come as a surprise to him. He could see how thin I'd got, and had been trying to find out the truth for some time. I'd been scared that he might reject me if I told him that I was still making myself sick.

'I'm still ill,' I said at last. 'I make myself sick.'

'When?' he asked.

'All the time. After every meal, pretty much.' I waited for him to step back in disgust. He didn't.

'I'm so scared of getting fat,' I finally said and burst into tears.

He just said, 'I'll always think you're beautiful, however you look,' and put his arms around me.

I think he thought that would put me at my ease and I'd immediately start to get better. In a way I did begin to improve my eating from then on, but it was a long road ahead.

From that time, Tom was on the lookout for signs. He wanted me to admit if I'd been sick. He didn't criticize me for doing it, he just said he didn't want me to keep it a secret. But keeping secrets was my life. I'd learned to be secretive about the Fellowship, my true feelings and my eating habits. It was not going to be easy. It had taken me a year to tell Tom that I was still bulimic.

Chapter Thirty-One

Pleased to Meet Me

About six months before I met Tom, he had made attempts to buy a house near Cambridge. The deal didn't go through, so soon after we started our relationship, he began mulling over the idea of buying a house in Norwich. It seemed that it was meant to be, because eight months after we met he found a suitable terraced property for sale in the city. We went to view it together and he showed me the house, almost opposite, where he had lived ten years previously, when he attended Norwich Institute to study sculpture.

I didn't say much as we poked around the rooms, but inside I felt excited. I started to let myself believe that Tom really had faith in our relationship. This realization astonished me. I was so mentally unstable – not to mention an ex-Fellowship girl.

The contract completed quickly, and by March 2001 it had all gone through, but Tom continued to live in his shared house in Cambridge as it made his commute to work easier. Instead, he got a lodger, Adam. But after a couple of months of Tom and I meeting up at the house at weekends he said, 'Why don't you move in?' I didn't give it a second's thought.

'Yes, I'd like that,' I replied.

Adam decided to move on not long after I settled in and I felt really enthusiastic about using the spare room to do all the creative things, like sewing, that I'd done with Mum as a child. But without Tom there to give me a sense of purpose, or the idea that I was working to serve God in some way, I just couldn't find the motivation to do much at all. The only consolation for me was that I was able to enforce my unhealthy eating routines without Adam, Tom or the knowing eye of Christine around to judge me for it.

Hardly any time passed at all before I was calling Tom every evening. I must have asked him a thousand times, in utter desperation, 'Will I ever be free of this?' He said I would. He had faith. If my thoughts about food and my body had let up for more than a second, I might have believed him, but from morning to night they were always there, filling my mind, leaving no space for anything else. And when, on rare occasions, they subsided just enough for me to feel a glimmer of hope, that hope would be cruelly crushed as they returned with renewed vigour. I felt like a prisoner of my own mind, and longed for an escape. I became suicidal.

'I just can't find the reason I need for living. What's the point of life?' I asked Tom despairingly.

'The point is to enjoy yourself,' he replied.

'But I don't know what I like doing,' I screamed back. 'I never had the chance to find out when I was a child. I wasn't allowed.

'I've got no sense of who I am. I look in the mirror and I don't know who the person is that looks back at me.'

'You define yourself by what you like and don't like,' Tom answered.

'I like doing art,' I said, remembering the projects Victor and I had worked on when I was a little girl, and how fun it had been.

'OK,' Tom said encouragingly, 'get yourself on a course.'

I started a part-time art course at the local college, an introduction to all the basic techniques, but the minute I walked into the room I knew it wasn't going to be easy. The hardest thing for me was being in the class with the other people. I immediately felt like the little girl, the outsider, who had been so lost at school all those years ago.

Much to my horror, I found myself hating a student who was not afraid to parade her work proudly and risk criticism. How I wished I could be like her.

I was on the brink of giving up when, one day, the head of art popped in and said my string prints were the best work in the class. This was just the sort of confidence boost my fragile ego needed. After that I relaxed a bit, and even made friends with my nemesis. Towards the end of the course, I found a picture by David Hockney, and fell in love with his work. Just using printing techniques, I recreated my version of his painting, which I really enjoyed doing.

I left the course with a great report, but the one thing I still didn't dare do was draw. Printing was OK, but I had no trust in my ability with a pencil. Tom persuaded me to give drawing a chance, saying that he'd help me, and for the next six months I worked at it continually. Every picture I started was a battle, and I'd often tear the paper to shreds in frustration and anger. Eventually, I became confident enough to tackle still lifes, and made him groan with my unflattering sketches of him. But, just as I was getting good, I gave it up.

My pleasure had turned into an obsession, which killed the enjoyment for me. I just couldn't do what Tom had advised and enjoy things without there having to be a point to them. Just as I wanted to be thinner than everyone else as an anorexic, I now wanted to be better than everyone else as an artist. I became more and more frustrated with myself, and angry that my life was being ruined by this relentless mental illness which made me so obsessive.

Diane had taught me to punch the cushions as an outlet for my anger, but I had another idea. I tried learning to play the drums, took weekly lessons and even bought my own kit. I liked the physicality of hitting the skins really hard. But I couldn't relax enough to play properly and gave up. A pattern was emerging.

Chapter Thirty-Two

Big Girl in a Short Skirt

I realized that I needed distraction from my negative thoughts and that sitting around at home was doing nothing to help me recover from my illness. My job as a Steiner assistant was only for a few hours a week and not nearly enough to keep me occupied. I started looking for full-time paid work, but was worried that my lack of education would make it hard for me to get a job, so I was delighted when I was employed by Julian Graves, a shop selling dried fruit, nuts and sweets.

The store was located in Norwich train station and most of the time I sat alone, in the empty shop, watching people scuttling past to catch their train, or flinging their arms around friends and family who welcomed them home.

Having vacuumed the floor and wiped the shelves which never seemed to need restocking, I felt overwhelmed by boredom. 'You must make the most of this,' I kept telling myself, 'you're lucky to have a job.' But somehow I didn't feel lucky. I hated myself for having messed up my chances to get qualifications at school and college, which could have led on to different career opportunities. I blamed myself.

'If I can get better from my eating disorder then I can go back to college,' I thought. I decided to throw myself into putting my anorexia behind me once and for all. I binged on nuts and sweets in the shop and piled my plate high with food in the evenings at home. The wild negative rants in my head persisted, unceasingly, and at work I vomited into the bin, disgusted at myself, while the trains screeched and whistled just a few feet away from me. At night I strode the two-mile walk home, hoping to burn some calories.

I distracted myself from my increasing weight by watching television and sleeping. I stopped looking at myself in the mirror and wore androgynous clothes that were a size too large. By the summer of 2003 I had reached eleven stone, almost twice the weight I had sunk to seven years earlier.

My relationship with Tom became strained. I had lost my feeling of sexiness that I had had when I was thin, and I barely let Tom touch me. He often placed his hand on my stomach when we lay in bed, loving my new curves, but I always pulled away abruptly, remembering Mum's words, '… the fat bit is hanging down onto the bed, Lindsey.' I felt like a ten-year-old child restrained in a womanly body that I didn't know what to do with. I desperately wanted to be thin again, but I also wanted freedom from my illness.

Tom and I decided to go on holiday with our friends, Martin and Lucy, and I welcomed the chance to escape from the shop, where I was working full time. I also hoped that it would be a chance for me and Tom to rekindle our relationship somehow.

* * *

Lucy, who had been to Florence before, booked the hotel for us, just a couple of hundred yards from the iconic domed cathedral. We had a great rooftop room, with French doors opening up onto a long balcony stretching all the way around the building.

The space had been made into a roof garden, with vines and climbers grown from huge terracotta pots, up over wood and wire frames. We spent the evenings sitting beneath the canopy, drinking wine at a little table outside our room, as the hotel staff hosed the plants with cooling water that ran over our feet. We had a fantastic view of the city and down to the busy streets far below.

The best day we had was in Siena, a train ride away. Like Florence, the main thoroughfares were packed with tourists, but we only had to duck down an alleyway or two to find some beautiful medieval streets. The whole city was built on a hill overlooking the rolling Tuscan countryside, just as we had imagined it to be before our visit.

It should all have been a wonderful experience, and my friends said, 'It sounds like you had a great holiday,' when I told them what we'd done, but all the time I was there my negative thoughts about my body never let up. I was socializing with great company, eating out, drinking – everything I had worked so hard to be free to do – but was still hopelessly unable to engage with my surroundings or enjoy what I had in front of me.

We travelled just as the 2003 European heat wave was starting, which led to the deaths of thousands of people. In Amsterdam I had been stick thin and could not get warm. This time the crippling Italian heat meant I was sweating constantly, which made me even more full of hate and aware of my insulating layers of flesh.

* * *

In a shop near our hotel in Florence, Tom saw a short skirt and said he thought I'd look great in it. He persuaded me to buy it, and I wore it for him, but I found it difficult. I was in two minds, one thinking I was sexy, the other believing that I looked absolutely revolting, I really thought that everyone was laughing at my efforts to look like a woman. Tom said I looked great, but I was so worried about what everyone else was thinking that I didn't care.

I returned home, determined to lose some weight.

'Please don't,' Tom begged me. 'You know what happens when you start dieting.'

'No I must,' I was adamant.

'Look, why don't you do some exercise then at least you will feel better about your body, without having to diet,' Tom suggested.

I felt so full of aggression and pent up emotion, that I agreed this was a good idea. There was a martial arts academy near where we lived, so I rang up to find out some details about the classes.

'Come and drop in for a visit,' the lady on the phone said.

When I got there I was introduced to a humourless boy of about twelve years of age, who bowed to me and introduced himself as 'Mr Wigley'. I immediately felt ill at ease. I was instructed to take off my shoes and follow him into an office, where he pushed a pen in my hand and told me to fill out a questionnaire. I'd only been expecting to have a friendly chat, and had no idea why I was filling out a form, but I knew that the sooner I got it done the faster I could get out of there. As I scribbled away, he sat behind the desk tapping his pen, telling me that I would have to bow to everyone when I was enrolled.

Blimey, I thought. I've only just got out of a religious sect. I don't want to join another one!

I looked elsewhere and found a version of Wing Tchun called AutoDefense. This sounded much more up my street, as it was more about getting fit than becoming Bruce Lee.

I went for about a year, one evening a week, but I didn't learn much. Everything I was told went in one ear and out the other. I was paralysed with self-consciousness most of the time. The worst thing for me was working in pairs. A short, rotund bloke was there every week with his sons, and I dreaded the sessions in which I had to work with members of his family. One of the sons didn't know his own strength, and gave me a thumping every time. Worst of all was the dad, who stood on my foot one week and nearly broke it. I longed to be paired with the experienced members, so that I wouldn't look such a fool.

Another ill-fated idea was throwing the javelin. 'If you want something vigorous and outdoors, try track and field,' Tom suggested. I looked at the possibilities. I considered myself too heavy for jumping, and didn't want to run because my face would go red. Throwing a spear seemed to fit my physique perfectly, so I joined the training sessions and started my athletics career.

'Perhaps you should try shot put,' suggested my coach after months watching my abysmal throws repeatedly nose dive into the grass. My best was twelve metres. How embarrassing.

Chapter Thirty-Three

Living in Sin

Tom had been promising to move to Norwich for a long time but being a writer for a music technology magazine meant that his skills were very specific. If he'd been a teacher or something universal like that, perhaps there wouldn't have been a problem.

Tom became sick of the situation too. Every Monday, he'd get up and drive out of Norwich very early so that he could pass through all the major traffic hot spots before they got jammed up. After work, he drove to his parents' house nearby, where he stayed until Thursday. Then, on the Friday he'd dash out of work and attempt to beat the rush hour on his way to Norwich. At best, he'd arrive at seven p.m., but a lot of the time there'd be a jam caused by a crash, and he would have to cut down country roads just to get home.

On one occasion his car broke down on a darkened road. He had to flag someone down to use their phone, and wait for Martin to tow him to safety and give him a lift home. I usually left it to Tom to cook so that I could turn a blind eye to all the really tasty, but fattening, ingredients he used, but this was the one evening I'd decided to do a curry extravaganza comprising new potatoes and green beans fried in spices, dhal and a vegetable curry with rice.

It all took a lot of preparation, but I had it all planned out in advance, and timed it so that it would be piping hot when Tom arrived home from work. I'd specifically put the rice on to be cooked and ready at exactly seven p.m. I wanted to show that I loved him.

When he failed to stroll through the door at seven on the dot, I felt cross with myself for my reaction. I wanted to feel concerned about the things that a good girlfriend should feel concerned about when her boyfriend doesn't arrive home, like 'has he had a crash and is he lying at the edge of the road somewhere calling out my name'. But my overriding fear was for my carefully and lovingly prepared meal, which was now burning in the oven.

Then one day, in the early autumn, out of the blue, he said, 'I'm going to leave work. I've been saying I'd move up here for years now and I'm sick of saying that and not doing anything about it. I'll just become freelance. If it doesn't work, I'll just have to find a part-time job to cover the mortgage.'

Once it was said, it just became a matter of when. It took another couple of months for him to hand in his notice and work out his last month. We were both feeling really excited and talked about all the things we'd be able to do with our time.

My dream had come true.

'I want to move out,' I said two weeks after Tom had moved in.

Almost from the moment he'd arrived I felt tense. When I was with Tom, I never let my guard down, worried that, if

I did, he might see something he wouldn't like. Suddenly he was there all the time, and there was no time for me to relax. I became more secretive and, in turn, distant and irritable.

I could no longer hide away when I was in one of my foul moods. It was suffocating for me, and it took only a few days for me to reach breaking point.

Tom wasn't exactly furious, but he made his thoughts clear. He'd packed in a job many people would have given their right arm to do, without anything regular to replace it. By this time I was working full time as a multi-drop driver, having left Julian Graves, and without that income he would really struggle.

'Stay,' he said. 'Please give it a chance.'

I did stay and there were good days when I felt really connected with Tom, and it was great. I loved to watch him when he became animated about his music and listened while he played me new songs on his guitar. We watched films endlessly together, and I annoyed him with my lack of knowledge about the film stars.

'Don't you know who that is?' he'd ask disbelievingly.

I'd shake my head, hating the fact I didn't.

'Come on, you do know,' he'd persist.

'I don't, just tell me.'

'That's Robert De Niro, he was in *The Godfather* playing the young version of Marlon Brando's character. You know who Marlon Brando is, don't you?'

'No.'

'Come on, he was in that film, *Apocalypse Now.*'

'I don't remember that,' I'd say.

'We watched it just the other week. It had Harrison Ford, Robert Duvall, Dennis Hopper and Martin Sheen in it.'

'Who?' I'd ask, cringing in anticipation of his outraged reaction.

And so it would go on until he mentioned Patrick Swayze; then I was on home ground.

It was fine for Tom to tease me, but I felt deeply mistrustful of other people. The slightest thing could knock me and trigger a deeply depressive mood I could see no way of escaping. It could last a week, two weeks, or even months. Sometimes all it would take was a look a person gave me in the street.

I'd wonder what they meant by it. Can they see that I'm a Fellowship girl? I'd ask myself. Have I been found out? Are they disgusted by the way I look? Have I done something wrong?

These were the sorts of question that would race through my mind and I'd immediately look to control my food and weight to protect my vulnerability. And, of course, when I went out, there were thousands of people looking at me, saying things that seemed critical. I gave everyone the power to make me or break me.

I was still convinced there was a set of rules every worldly person was following, and I was showing myself up by breaking them in some way. I somehow felt that if I could find out the secret, learn the rules, I could fit in and ensure no one would criticize me.

Tom would tell me straight that there was no proper, worldly way to behave, and that there was nothing I could do to control how people thought about me. He said that I could only please some of the people some of the time. 'Some people will love you and others will hate you, whatever you do,' he repeated over and over.

It didn't matter how many times he said it, though. I still felt the same.

The managers of the courier company I was working for certainly didn't seem too keen on me. I came down with a cold and tried to plough on through it. I was so afraid of what they would think of me if I missed a day that I carried on when I should have called in sick. The cold turned into the flu and I had no choice. Tom warned me to rest up and tried to convince me that if I stayed in bed I'd recover more quickly. Still, I pushed myself to get up. After a week off, I was worse than ever and Tom had to take in a doctor's note for me, saying that I was unfit to work for another week.

When I returned, having had two weeks off, my clocking-in card was missing. I spoke to Steve, a man with a bullish attitude, who had grown fat from sitting behind a desk. He said that they didn't have so much work and I wasn't needed any more. In other words, I'd been fired.

I'd been there only a couple of months but it was just the sort of job I liked. Most of the day I was on my own, and my interactions with the customers were brief. In my van, speeding along the Norfolk country roads, I was closed off from the world outside, and could eat my food in private, whilst listening to the music I liked.

When my confidence returned, I started searching for a similarly solitary job and soon saw an advert for a Post Office collection driver. It was part-time, collecting from businesses and post offices in the city centre. I probably wouldn't have got the job if it hadn't been for my brief courier experience, so at least it hadn't been in vain. I was given a few days' training with an experienced driver, kitted up with some badly fitting clothes designed for ladies with humongous hips, and let loose in my red van.

In search of additional income, I decided to contact the Steiner Kindergarten to see if they needed me. They did, and I started running mother-and-toddler groups for children under three and a half. These were the same sessions as I had helped Rupert with before, but this time I was paid to run them myself with an assistant. Quite what the parents expected to get from me, a paranoid anorexic with empathy problems, I'm not sure, but they seemed happy to let me guide their offspring.

There was plenty they didn't know about me, that was certain, and there were even things I kept secret from Tom. I'd been with him four years before I finally confessed to my little habit of regurgitating my food into my mouth. I felt so ashamed and disgusted by it, that I thought he'd feel the same about *me* if he knew.

'Oh, right,' he said when I told him. 'Is that why your breath smells sometimes?'

I couldn't believe that was all he had to say. For years I had sat on the sofa next to him, watching TV, quietly bringing up and swallowing my food again, desperately hoping he wouldn't notice the odd dribble that escaped and ran down my chin.

'Yeah, that's why I hardly open my mouth when I kiss you. I was really scared that you would think I tasted horrible,' I replied.

'To be honest, I thought it was because you didn't like me.' Tom sounded relieved.

Just after Christmas, I said to Tom that I wanted to get a cat. I'm not sure why, but maybe my memories of my grandma's strays had popped into my head. Tom loved cats, having grown up with them in his house, so he didn't need much persuading. We headed to a cat-rescue home to take a look at some contenders.

The rescue home was actually the back garden of a cat fanatic, who had converted most of her property into a network of cages. We looked around, from cage to cage, but didn't feel attracted to any of the ones in view. We were about to leave when Tom pointed out a small tabby kitten crouching nervously in the corner of a cage, being closely guarded by another cat of the same size. Tom reached out his hand and it backed up as far as it could, spitting in fear. 'Let's get this one,' he said, and I agreed.

The problem was, we didn't have the heart to separate the two babies. They obviously looked after each other. We came home with two kittens, rescued from a farm where they were running wild together with fifty others. They were only five months old, incredibly cute, and totally undomesticated. We named the more confident one, the boy, Orwell, and the nervous girl Mog. Mog didn't seem right, though, so we started calling her Lady Cat, and it stuck.

For months they lived under the futon in the front bedroom where Tom had his office. Tom would tempt them out with some sliced ham and a game of catch the string, but it took a long time to gain their trust.

I had expected to feel love for them, but it didn't come. I could appreciate how cute they were, but found myself looking after them in a practical way without its going deeper than that. My windowsills were packed with seed trays and Lady Cat was constantly sitting on them. I would fly into a rage if I saw her climbing on the trays, and just couldn't empathize with the fear that she felt.

With growing horror it dawned on me that it wasn't just the cats that I couldn't love, but Tom too. I did all I could to look after his needs, cooking and cleaning for him, behaving like I thought a girlfriend should, but if I was really honest

with myself I had to admit I just didn't feel in love with
him.

It took me a lot longer to understand that you can't love
someone else when you don't love yourself.

Chapter Thirty-Four

The Baby Belly

Rather than confront Tom with my devastating realization, I blundered on, telling myself that I could, and would, love him if I worked harder at getting over my eating disorder. 'It's all my fault,' I thought. I wished that he had heeded the words I had said to him outside the pub four years previously. I had been right when I said, 'I'm fucked up.'

Our sexual relationship was more off than on, and we didn't use contraception. My periods had returned but I was so used to not worrying about getting pregnant, and not even sure that I could after years of being malnourished, that it hardly even occurred to me to do so.

So it came as a shock when I did fall pregnant.

My first reaction was utter elation that I wasn't infertile, but then I told Tom. He wasn't quite so happy. Only a few months earlier I'd been hellbent on moving out, so he was worried about our future and that of the baby. Tom was also concerned about work. He was struggling to establish himself as a freelancer and money was tight. Suddenly, there would be the added pressure of providing for a child.

I pushed his concerns aside, telling myself that if we split I'd bring the baby up on my own. I felt fairly superior to other parents already, having based my thinking on Steiner. 'How hard can it be?' I thought. 'If I process the baby using the methods I've learnt from Steiner, it will turn out to be the perfect being.' And I forgot about my worries about not being able to love, absolutely certain that I would fall in love with my baby as soon as I saw him or her.

I'd spent the last ten years trying to rid myself of any trace of a belly. It represented everything I hated about myself. If I ate food, that's the place I knew it was going, and when I got upset it would churn. But now it started to grow and, for once, I didn't mind. It somehow felt right. One day I felt something inside. Not a groan of hunger, twinge of a muscle or process of digestion. This was something I'd never felt before, but the mother in me knew it for what it was. As the weeks passed, it began to kick and press, moving around beneath my ribs.

I began to resent Tom, who was reluctant to touch me. He said it was because he didn't want to press on the baby and hurt it, but I took it to heart. No, that's not right. I took it to belly. Whoever said the heart was the centre of emotions? For me, an anorexic, it was my belly in every way. Now, finally, I was proud of it, and he seemed repelled. I knew he was cautious and didn't want to get excited in case it all went wrong, but I wished he'd just share my joy.

The months passed and my body stretched and stretched. I looked at myself naked in the mirror, turning this way and that, wondering about what the baby would be like. I'd already planned so much. I read books on pregnancy, child-birth and the early years. I left nothing to chance.

We started fighting, the baby and I. I'd be lying in bed, or trying to eat, when a foot or elbow would suddenly jab me in the side. 'Oi! Get back in there,' I'd say softly, pushing the tiny limb back to where it was more comfortable.

I revelled in being pregnant and didn't let it prevent me from doing anything. Five months in, Tom and I went on a camping holiday to the Yorkshire Dales. One day we hired mountain bikes and got lost. We ended up doing a fifty-mile round trip. We also played each other at squash every week, right up to within a month before my due date. I felt healthy and, in spite of an uncertain future with Tom, positive for the first time in my life.

Then, one day, out of the blue, I received a letter from my sister Alice. Contact with my parents had dwindled since they had returned to the Fellowship, although it had never ceased completely. The reason for this was there was a new 'Elect Vessel' who thought that the best way to keep the numbers of the sect from dwindling was to rekindle relationships with ex members, so the rule of no contact with Fellowship 'sinners' had been relaxed.

But I certainly wasn't expecting any kind of contact with Alice, who I hadn't seen since I was seven years old, nor spoken to since that fateful telephone conversation in 1991. I hadn't thought much about her at all in that time, if I'm honest. Her religion was obviously far more important to her than I or my welfare, and I had put her out of my mind.

I read her letter with a mixture of excitement and scepticism. She mentioned her family, three boys and a girl – my nephews and nieces. I remembered the joy at waiting to become an aunt at the age of six. I had felt so grown up. Now Timothy, her first born, was eighteen years old. She mentioned the phone call I had made, saying she had cried when she put the phone down and wished we could have had the conversation all over again so she could do it differently.

Now that I was pregnant with my own child, my attitude towards my family had hardened. It appalled me that anyone could choose to stay faithful to the rules of a religion rather than stand by their own flesh and blood. As far as I was concerned she had shown her true colours. But my interest was raised. Who the hell was this person who called herself my sister? She also included a photo of her and her children. Tom and I laughed at this, as they were so obviously Fellowship members, in their long skirts and headscarves, short-sleeved shirts and slacks. It was almost a relief to be reminded, because, in spite of my scorn for them, I felt the same old pull when I thought about my lost family. This very evident uniform that they wore so obediently was a stark reminder for me of the more sinister side of the Fellowship.

Alice followed the letter with a phone call. Mum had rung me and asked if I would be willing to talk to her. 'Of course,' I said. No hesitation.

The moment I heard her voice I was transported back to childhood. It still sounded exactly the same, and what was more of a shock was the fact that mine sounded just like hers! Our beliefs and the years may have put a massive division between us, but the fact that we were family was undeniable.

So what did being family mean to her? Quite evidently, not what it meant to me. She showed little or no interest in me or my life, enquiring only if I wanted money. Money for what? Was this a bribe or a promise? I felt disgust and the phone call was brief. I had had so much experience of genuine love from Tom and my new worldly friends that I could view her efforts only as a cynical move on the part of the Fellowship to try to entice me back.

Next came the Bible. It arrived 'with love' from Alice. I put it straight back in the envelope it came in and posted it to Alice. I couldn't bear for one moment to have such an item in my house. It was their rule book, the book that told them to reject me. It made me feel sick.

But then I received the offer of something more enticing. Mum asked if I wanted to go and visit them again, and meet Alice and her kids. Well, this I could not turn down. I was simply too curious.

Of course, this time I wouldn't be able to stay with them, so I arranged to stay with Victor the night before the visit, the plan being to drive over to Mum's in the morning.

I felt really nervous during the journey to see them. Not only was I going to meet my sister, but I hadn't seen my mum and dad and Samantha since they returned to the Fellowship. Would they be different? I really knew then what they mean when they say 'butterflies in the stomach'.

I had told her about the pregnancy over the telephone but I couldn't wait for her to see the evidence for herself. Her baby, with a baby of its own.

I arrived at Mum's house just in time for lunch. I was invited to stay, but was told I had to eat in the kitchen – on my own. I sat on a bar stool, pulled up to the narrow work-top and read Dad's *Telegraph* while listening to the chat and laughter from my parents and Samantha having their meal in the dining room. I didn't really feel that I wanted to be with them this time. I almost felt superior, as if I were some-one special for having made the right choice, and they were weak for rejoining the Fellowship just because of one very long-overdue apology. One apology for twenty years of agony? It made my blood boil, and I used that anger to deal with the simple fact that I felt subhuman sitting there in the kitchen on my own.

After lunch, Mum drove me to Alice's house. Mum, Samantha and I had driven past it so many times after we were 'withdrawn from', just hoping for a glimpse of her in the driveway, or heading out to do the shopping. Now I was actually going inside. As I arrived, Alice stepped outside onto the drive with a big smile on her face. It was peculiar. I knew her and I didn't know her at the same time. So familiar and yet a stranger. This situation was going to be far worse than I'd anticipated. However did I think I could breeze in, unaffected by these people? What the hell was I trying to prove? I couldn't back out now, though.

I smiled back, a little stiffly, I suspect, but declined her offer of a hug. Bizarrely enough, she took me on a tour of her home, introducing every room. Perhaps she really wanted me to see where she had lived her life all of these past years, or maybe it was just that she wanted to avoid the awkwardness of not being able to offer me a drink.

I was introduced to my nephews and niece. I stood looking at them, not knowing what to say to these kids who in another life, another world, would have been greeted with a hug and a kiss from their Auntie Lindsey.

An unbearable silence fell over us. 'I shouldn't be here,' I thought to myself, and told my sister it was time for me to leave.

I had decided to visit Natalie while I was in the area, and Alice drove me to her house. I went straight from one world into another. I think I hoped that there would be a chat over a cup of tea and some reminiscences over old times. But, of course, I wasn't the only one who had grown up and changed. Natalie had changed, too, and it was hard to find the joy again that I had felt and we'd shared when I was a kid.

I found out she was suffering from depression. This made me feel bad. I had used her as my lifeline to a more sane existence when I was a little girl, and now I minded that I had obviously missed being there for her when some bad things were going on in her life. The funny thing was, in some ways our relationship was the same. She looked to me now for advice on how to recover from depression and mental illness, believing that I was over all my problems. If only she knew the truth.

Having realized that my meeting with Alice had not had the desired effect, the Fellowship finally gave up on me. The priests, who were the brother and dad of Gareth, the boy whom I had caught with his trousers undone all those years ago, and had longed to marry, wrote to me stating that my relationship with Tom was contrary to scripture and I had to make a decision about whether I was going back. It wasn't a last-ditch effort to pair me up with Gareth and his willy: they just needed to know so that they could formally make me 'withdrawn from'. Apparently, Samantha and I had only been granted the status of 'shut up' as we were too young to be responsible for our actions when my parents and Victor were 'withdrawn from'. I didn't reply to the letter. What was there to say? I no longer viewed the situation as 'us and them'. As far as I was concerned, I was Lindsey, no label needed or attached. I had learned that the world doesn't compartmentalize people. That was a Fellowship thing, and I was learning not to see myself as an ex-member.

Dad rang me a couple of weeks later, saying they needed an answer. I refused to give one. He said they would have to make the decision for me, and I replied that it made no difference to me what they did or didn't do.

I spoke to Mum on the phone a few days before the first birthday I celebrated since they had returned to the Fellowship. No mention was made of it. I didn't want to have to prompt Mum and remind her of her youngest daughter's special day! Mum commented that she had posted some Sainsbury's vouchers to me and then we said goodbye. Sure enough, a day or so before the big day the vouchers arrived. I had wondered if she had sent them as a birthday present but had forgotten to state their meaning. I soon dismissed this idea. There was no card in with the vouchers and no mention of a birthday. The day passed.

A couple of days later I again spoke to Mum. Again I did not talk of the birthday and neither did she. It was then that it hit me. This was a deliberate avoidance of the date of my birth. In effect, by ignoring the most significant date of my life she was, I suddenly realized with despair in my heart, doing her best to ignore my existence. Her duty as a mother was demonstrated in her actions, but in her heart, I believe, I had died. A part of me died that day too. It was a relief to return home to Tom, to normality.

As the weeks ticked by, and various health visitors and midwives popped in to take measurements and leave information packs, the due date got ever nearer. Tom was desperately trying to finish off some of the most important DIY jobs, while I started buying baby things.

The due date of our baby came, and then it went. Nothing happened. It was the same again the next day, and the next. Our lovely midwife kept in close contact and reassured us that it was OK. But still the days passed and nothing happened. We began to wonder if it was real. In some ways the waiting was like being 'shut up' or even 'withdrawn from'. We were just waiting for something to happen, but without any idea when it would. And, when I was a whole week past the due date, it started to feel as if the wait would go on for ever.

The midwife told us that exercise, semen and curry were things that can bring on labour, so we went for a walk, had sex and an Indian, although probably not in that order. Still nothing.

It was a cold, damp afternoon when I started to feel a few regular pains. I'd had the Braxton Hicks – or false labour – on one or two occasions before, and this felt similar but somehow different at the same time. We allowed ourselves to feel a little excited, and, after an hour or two, decided to do another walk. Unlike the Braxton Hicks I was used to, the pains got stronger and spread all over my belly.

Outside there was a mist and the cold air felt fresh. We headed off on one of our favourite routes, down towards the river, and then up towards the heath on the hill. Everywhere seemed quiet, as if the whole city were waiting too. Back home I called Carol and told her that I thought the baby was coming. She asked me a few questions about what I felt and then said she'd be round in a couple of hours' time.

It was somewhere around nine p.m., when Carol arrived, armed with surgical gloves, a blood-pressure monitor and stethoscope.

'You're in the early stages of labour,' she announced enthusiastically. Carol was always full of energy, despite being on call at all hours. The baby was already a week overdue, so she recommended doing a membrane sweep, which would get things moving more quickly. This all happened on the sofa in the living room, while Tom paced around in the back room. Carol left us with some advice, telling me to call when the contractions really kicked in. Then it was back to waiting. Something big was about to happen and yet our house and street fell quiet.

We didn't go to bed that night. Sometime around midnight, dressed in my nightie with the intention of catching some sleep, I found myself doubled up in pain, face down in the sofa. The pain came in waves, first every couple of minutes, then every minute. Tom looked at his stopwatch to find out if it was time to make the call to the midwives.

By this time Tom had dug the foam camping mat out from under the stairs, placing it under my sore, bare knees. We had a wood floor, so at least we didn't have to worry about ruining a carpet!

In the early hours, the pain increased dramatically and I was yelling out in agony. I'm not sure what the neighbours heard through the walls, but I was already beyond caring. I barked curt instructions to Tom, who knelt beside me, rubbing my back. With each wave I squeezed tight on his hand, sinking my nails into his skin.

The first pair of midwives arrived at about one a.m. I didn't move or look round. Carol was off shift, so the women were both strangers. 'This is Lindsey,' Tom said, introducing the back of my head.

'Pleased to meet you, Lindsey, how are you getting on?'

'Aaaaaaaaaaaaaaaaaaaagh!' I screamed.

I may have managed to look up once during the two hours or so that they were there, but the rest of the time I just heard voices.

Everyone was telling me to lay off the gas for as long as possible. Apparently, the more you take the less effect it seems to have. That was easier said than done, though, and, as soon as I had that bit between my teeth, I was sucking the bottle as if my life depended on it. I certainly felt as though it did. So great was my appetite for that precious pain reliever, I got through the canister in no time, and was on to a second one. My gentle home-birth plan was starting to matter less and less. All I wanted was pain relief, whatever form it came in.

Then bottle number two developed a leaky valve. From within my blurry daze I could hear the midwives calling some colleagues who were on another 'job' nearby, to see if they had any spares. Meanwhile, Tom went looking for a spanner in a desperate attempt to tighten the seal. It was madness!

I heard the door swing open again, revealing my behind to any milkmen or early-morning dog walkers who might happen to be passing. There were now two teams of midwives in the house, clanking around with bags, swapping gas bottles. I couldn't move my head an inch. Sweat was pouring off me and I was delirious with pain, dehydration and tiredness. In this state, the midwives were able to do anything they liked to me for the purpose of checking that things were going smoothly. Various instruments were inserted here and there, listening to the baby's heartbeat and checking blood pressures. I didn't care what they stuck in me, but there was no way on earth I was going to move.

'Where's the gas?' I screamed at Tom every forty seconds as a new wave hit. The bit was usually right beside my head on the sofa, but my eyes were so full of salty sweat that I couldn't see a thing. Hours of the same thing passed, until another midwife shift came to an end and a new lot arrived. By this time I must have used up all the gas supplies in Norwich and was as high as a kite.

'Never again, I'm never doing this again. I can't take any more. Help me, please, Tom. I don't want to do this, I can't. I've had enough.' These were the only things I could say. Tom looked at me helplessly.

'That's great. Four centimetres dilated,' Carol said to Tom as she removed a rubber glove. She was back on shift.

'Is that good?' he asked.

'It needs to get to about ten centimetres, so we're making good progress,' Carol replied reassuringly.

'So how long will that take?' he asked again.

'It's taking about one centimetre an hour.'

There was no response. We'd been leaning over the sofa all night and Tom had just worked out that I still had at least six hours to go. If he'd had a chance, I think Tom would have started on a gas bottle himself.

Carol had really taken to me before the birth. She was so supportive of my plan to have a home birth and wanted it to be the serene and spiritual event I'd described to her. As a lot of people do, I think she thought I was a really nice, sweet girl and deserved a matching experience.

'Get me to hospital now! Cut it out! Fucking cut me open and get this fucking thing out of me, now!' I screamed.

'Lindsey!' Tom said.

'Give me an epidural; just stick the fucking needle in me now. I can't take any more, I've fuckin' had enough.' I said things that would make a squaddie blush, and then worse.

I was still demanding to be rushed to hospital for my epidural and Caesarean as the midwives ran me a warm bath and somehow managed to get me through the back room and kitchen into the bathroom. They ordered Tom upstairs to grab an hour or so of badly needed sleep, reassuring him that there was a way to go still, and he wouldn't miss anything.

An hour later I was back in the living room again, swearing to high heaven and guzzling another gas bottle until my gums were bleeding. Tom reappeared and suddenly things seemed to be moving again. My body had taken a rest. It knew what it was doing, readying itself for the finale. By now it was early afternoon.

'You've got to start pushing, Lindsey,' Carol began saying. 'The baby's getting tired and it's time to push it out. Breathe and push, breathe and push.'

'I can't push,' I whimpered. I was so exhausted.

They all started offering words of encouragement. For some reason to do with changing shifts, there were four midwives and a student in the room, all sitting around in a semicircle observing the state of my behind.

'Yes, I can see the head, keep going Lindsey, you're doing fantastically well.'

'What's happening, what can you see?' asked Tom, who was by my side stroking my head and back and having his hand crushed by mine.

'Come round to this end and have a look,' one of the women said chirpily, and started pointing out to Tom the way I was bulging underneath.

Then, suddenly, I felt this incredible urge to push take over me. I knew what to do, it felt right.

'Here it comes,' a midwife said, and they all immediately began busying themselves, putting out towels and plastic sheets.

Nina had been in my belly for a long time, and was eager to get on with her life. Even before her shoulders and body emerged, her blue face wrinkled up, she coughed up some liquid and began to cry.

My limp body was manoeuvred carefully so that I was sitting on my terribly sore behind. Then this tiny creature was placed in my arms. This was the moment I'd been waiting for. The moment when all the pain of the previous eighteen hours would fade into nothingness, the moment I'd be filled with a total and unconditional love for my beautiful baby.

I looked down at her tiny body, and waited for it to hit me. I felt nothing. Emptiness. This wasn't how it was supposed to be.

Chapter Thirty-Five

Don't I Want You, Baby?

I'd expected my first few weeks with a baby to be the best of my life, but they were some of the worst. Part of the problem was that, in the nine months leading up to the birth, I'd had plenty of time to fantasize about how it was going to be. I had everything mapped out in my head.

I'd read all of the mother-and-baby books I could lay my hands on and, from that, decided when it was best to feed Nina, and how to organize her sleeping patterns. I left nothing to chance; I intended to be the perfect mum, the idea being that the process would result in the perfect child. I had terry towels instead of disposable nappies; I would reason with the child rather than resort to smacking; and bottle feeding was definitely not going to happen.

My plan seemed perfect. If there was one thing I was really good at, it was planning, and Nina was the ideal project. She was a blank canvas, and I intended to paint my own picture, in my style.

The trouble was, my plan was far, far from perfect. I'd overlooked one important thing that turned everything upside down. It was Nina herself. From the moment she popped out, she knew exactly how she expected things to be done. If Tom and I thought we were determined individuals, we were about to be shown what determination really was. As my schedules crumbled in a pathetic heap, I immediately started thinking that I was a failure as a parent.

To make matters worse, breastfeeding was proving to be really difficult. Surely it was the most natural thing in the world? Apparently not.

It got off to a bad start. I was supposed to feed her every few hours in the night. I'm not sure if I knew this or was too tired to remember, but at first it didn't happen. By the time the midwives had cleared up, made their notes and prepared us some toast and hot tea, it was early evening. They tucked me up in bed with Nina and headed home. All three of us were absolutely exhausted. Tom and I decided to start as we meant to go on and put Nina in the tiny cot in the cosy box room next to ours. Even in that space she seemed ridiculously small. Then, we all slept.

The thing was, on her first day in the world, Nina had been left without milk for nine hours. Later that day, we all had to drive over to the hospital for some official baby checks. The nurse tested all her joints and reflexes, then stripped her off to be weighed. Rather worryingly, she'd shed about eight ounces overnight. The nurse said this was not uncommon, but it still made us all the more anxious to get some food into Nina as quickly as possible.

I tried for hours, but Nina just would not latch on. You'd think that the nipple would simply go in the mouth and that would be it. Not so. A midwife stopped by and threw me some advice. Then our health visitor checked in to find out how things were going. I was tearful and tired, so she helped me reposition Nina on my lap so that she would feed. It was all about getting the nipple up to the roof of the mouth. If it didn't go in right, the baby could not suck properly and simply started biting hard. In no time at all, both nipples were so sore that feeding was agony. And, each time, there was more biting than feeding. What little milk went in seemed to come straight back out again.

In those early days, we were visited almost every day by either a midwife or our health visitor. All sorts of measurements were taken and questions asked. It was clear that Nina was gaining weight, so something must have been going in, but it was too little. I called the number I'd been given for a breastfeeding counsellor, who gave me her advice. I was confused. What she said differed from what the health visitor was advising, and that was not the same as I'd been told by the midwives. Everyone was telling me something different, while Nina was frantic with hunger.

My nipple pain turned to agony, which spread all over my chest. It felt as if I had the flu, I was shivering and shaking so much. I got furious with Nina, furious with myself, and Tom got his share of the blame, too.

I'd developed mastitis, which is an infection caused by blocked milk ducts, and was diagnosed as having thrush – a side effect of an antibiotic prescription – which spread to Nina's tiny mouth, covering the inside with painful sores. No wonder she was having trouble feeding.

Sleeping was not something Nina was keen to do, either. She certainly had not the slightest interest in following my plan. God, she was a petulant baby! It seemed as though she'd wake up after every hour of sleep, and then the ordeal of getting her latched on would begin.

While all this was going on, I was asking myself a question: Why don't I feel unconditional love for her? I'd failed to love her, and now I was failing to feed her. I'd wanted to be a better mum than all those others I saw shouting at their children or stuffing dummies or bottles in their mouths to keep them quiet. Now I felt like the worst parent in the world. Tom tried his best to reassure me, but his logical reasoning just irritated me even more.

I began to resent this child that was messing up my best-laid plans. Who the hell did she think she was? Didn't she know what was good for her? Then there was the constant crying.

Gradually, day by day, Nina started to break me. Tom's advice had always been to go with the flow. He hated all those books on bringing up the baby, saying that you have to see what sort of child you've got, and then do what's best for it, not try to change the child to fit your own ideas. The trouble was that I just couldn't let go. I'd learned to control the way I behaved at school so that I'd be accepted; I'd controlled my food so that my body would look a certain way; and now I was compelled to control this baby.

I had a lot to learn, and Nina was about to give me a long, hard lesson.

Sometimes I felt really desperate for help. Tom's parents lived a few hours' drive away, so it wasn't as if his mum could drop by and help out in the week. She had never learned to drive, so Sundays, when his dad was around, were the only times they could visit. As I was breastfeeding it meant that no one, not even Tom, could take over, not for long, anyway.

'Where are you when I need you, Mum?' I whispered to myself as I rocked Nina in my arms. I felt so alone; desperately lonely.

I yearned for Mum, and several times very nearly picked up the telephone to call her. But each time my hand hovered over the receiver, I pulled myself back. What kind of help could she give me? And another more sinister thought crept into my mind. What if she saw my neediness as a sign that I couldn't cope with Nina and tried to take her away from me?

But I couldn't cope.

Tom was concerned about my frantic state and said if I really wanted to call Mum, it wouldn't do any harm. So I did.

'Leave Nina to cry,' was her advice. 'She's got to learn that you are in control, not her.'

After one night of listening to our baby daughter in distress, Tom and I vowed we would never leave her to cry again.

I finally snapped one evening. 'I haven't even hung up the washing I did this morning,' I screamed at Tom. 'I can't do anything because she doesn't let me put her down.'

I rang Mum the next day. 'Please help,' I begged her, 'I need you.'

'I'll try and get permission from the priests to come and see you,' she promised. I couldn't believe it. Mum wanted to help me? My excitement at possibly seeing her again, and relief swept aside my doubts that I had done the right thing in asking for her aid.

I waited eagerly for her to call with the answer to her request.

'I can come,' she said when she rang.

A Fellowship family living in Norwich agreed to accommodate Mum and Dad so that they could stay for three days and could attend all the local meetings.

When they turned up at our house, it was as if they were a team of professionals, ready to get their job done. They were clearly keen to see Nina, but made sure their friendly interaction with Tom and me didn't go beyond basic pleasantries. Everything else we spoke about was to do with managing the baby. Mum kept her headscarf on the whole time, and both refused the offer of a drink and food.

Once Dad had dropped Mum off, he disappeared, leaving her to pass on her knowledge. He turned up again at lunchtime and whisked her away so that she could have a drink and food. I accepted their behaviour; I was just glad to be with Mum.

Over those three days, she cleaned the house top to bottom, and taught me how to bathe Nina, and I even managed to get out of the house for a short time while she babysat. All the time Mum was there, Tom was working from home. It must have been odd for him, having this be-scarved, focused and determined woman organizing the house, but declining his hospitality. He got on with work as much as possible to avoid the situation. Having grown up with Mum and Dad's ways, there was a part of me that saw them as normal. To Tom, though, it was confusing.

'It's just so weird,' Tom commented during the evening of the first day of their visit.

'They won't even drink a glass of water in my house, which feels like an insult, but they actually seem to like me, and act as if it's all perfectly normal.'

'They don't have anything against you personally,' I said, 'it's just that you're worldly; not one of them, so you're inconsequential in their lives. That's what Dad was telling you when you first met.'

'I'm the dad of their granddaughter,' he insisted.

'Doesn't matter. Look at how they view me. Now I'm out of the Fellowship, I may as well be a stranger.'

Mum was happy to have long but practical conversations with Tom about what I should be doing with Nina, and they got on really well in a way. But there was a strict unspoken boundary, which Tom just had to accept, because it was non-negotiable.

The same was true with Dad. After discussing the traffic on the roads and the weather, Dad would politely say, 'So, Tom, how's work?' Tom worked on a computer, writing about music technology, which are both things that aren't accepted by the Fellowship. If only he'd been a chartered accountant!

After Mum went home, I tried to follow the routines she had recommended. I used the dummy that she had bought for Nina and did as she said, forcing it into my baby's mouth when she struggled to spit it out. 'Don't let her control you,' Mum had said, again, and I tried not to. But somehow the more I tried, the less comfortable I felt with her advice. I reminded myself that she had never been the most demonstrative of mums in terms of showing me physical affection and as a little girl I'd had to work to soften her hard edges.

I'd climb on her lap, sitting on her knitting so she had to stop working and hug me. I'd come up to her from behind, throw my arms around her, and squeeze until she gasped. I think I forced her love for me from her, rather than it flowing out naturally, but I needed the loving and wouldn't let up until I had it.

Despite Mum's no nonsense approach to childcare, it wasn't the last time I asked her for help. I spoke to her on the phone regularly, sometimes just to get some practical advice, other times just because I needed the comfort of her supportive words.

I knew that my guilt for not loving Nina was driving me to over compensate in my motherly actions as I threw myself into looking after her. If she made the slightest noise I'd jump up, filled with anxiety, trying to serve her every want. I was just desperate for her not to know my awful secret. The thought that she might sense my lack of love plagued me constantly.

Nevertheless my determination to breastfeed crumbled just four weeks after she was born. Nina wasn't gaining weight particularly fast, my nipples felt as though I'd been feeding an angry cobra, and I couldn't even remember what sleep was. I reluctantly bought some bottles and formula milk and introduced Tom to his new job. I still breastfed her as I couldn't bear the thought of giving up, but the bottle at least gave me a chance to fill her up so that she'd settle a little more easily.

Tom was always coming up with nicknames for people. Most of the time they were affectionate, and he had plenty for Nina. Nina Noo, Nooie and Bubster were just a few. But he also started calling her the Two-Foot Tyrant. She certainly seemed like one a lot of the time and, though I knew it was probably my fault, a result of my over-anxious attentions, she had us running around night and day. A more passive child might have complied with my feeding and sleeping schedules earlier on, but almost from the start Nina was having none of it.

If she was awake, there was no putting her down. No toys could hold her attention for more than a second, so even plonking her down on a play mat while I nipped to the toilet was near impossible.

I bought myself a baby sling, so that I could at least get a few things done with her in it. It might not have been something health-and-safety types would have approved of, because I was often frying the dinner with Nina strapped to my breast.

Nighttimes were hard, too. We tried everything to get Nina to settle. Putting her in our bed, so that she could grab a bite to eat whenever it suited her, sometimes worked, but, more often than not, she'd spend the whole time fidgeting about. In her white babygrow she looked like a little grub, wriggling away, so Tom added Grubster to the list of nicknames. When I got really desperate for sleep, Tom would take our little grub downstairs, climb into a sleeping bag and try to get her to sleep in the crook of his arm, her head resting on his chest. It may have taken him hours to get her to lie still, but some sleep was better than none.

Five months after the birth, my maternity leave ended and I went back to Royal Mail, collecting post in my red van. I'd started it a week before the due date, but Nina was a week late, so two had passed even before she arrived. I didn't tell anyone that I felt relieved to be back at work. I was working only part-time at the Post Office, two and a half hours each afternoon and Saturday morning, but I lived for those hours when Tom would take over looking after Nina. My worry about not loving her exhausted me as much as the physical drain on my body from lack of sleep. Instinctively I knew that Tom was the better parent, more relaxed and more loving, and I was glad that he and Nina spent so much time together. He carried Nina around in a strap-on baby carrier. A muslin cloth was draped over the front to catch her dribble, and Tom would walk everywhere with his hands in front so Nina could hold onto his index fingers, as if they were motorbike handlebars. 'She'll be all right,' I thought, as long as she has her dad.

Chapter Thirty-Six

Unfinished Business

During the first year of Nina's life my constant worrying about my lack of love for her gradually subsided. Going back to work had made me feel less trapped and given me time to relax, which helped me feel less stressed when I was with her. As the months passed and her personality shone through I began to admire and like her spirited ways. She reminded me of myself, obstinate and stubborn, and this recognition helped me feel better about myself. 'How can I hate myself so much when my daughter is so similar to me?' I thought often. I may as well be saying I hated Nina, and I most definitely didn't.

But as so often happened, when one worry disappeared, I replaced it with another.

When Nina was just over a year old I announced again to Tom that I was leaving.

'This time I mean it,' I stated firmly. 'I don't love you.'

I really thought I didn't. Now that I had felt more affectionate towards Nina, it seemed logical to me that, if I didn't feel love for Tom, it was because we weren't right for each other.

'I got all the way to thirty-two without having a baby, and now I finally have one you want to take it away,' Tom said.

'You can still see her, you're her dad,' I replied.

'I don't want to be some distant figure, replaced by some other bloke who she eventually thinks of as Dad,' he went on.

I became impatient, saying, 'But surely you can see how awful our relationship is?'

My pregnancy with Nina had acted as a distraction from the difficulties Tom and I were having in our relationship. But we had drifted apart since she was born, partly because I had been filled with concerns about my relationship with Nina. Every time Tom tried to tell me about his work, or talk about something which didn't involve our daughter, I'd hardly engage with him.

Now there was a distance between us, but I refused to accept it was my fault. I suppose I was fed up with blaming myself for all the problems we had.

'If only you felt better about yourself,' Tom would say, 'then you'd feel better about us.'

This comment began to infuriate me. I felt at the mercy of my eating disorder and would scream back at him, 'You don't know how hard this is for me.'

Whereas once I had felt safe and secure with him looking after me, it now felt like a noose around my neck. I desperately wanted to prove that I didn't need him, mainly because deep inside I knew that I relied on him too heavily. Without him I felt empty, but I knew that I wasn't going to find myself if I stayed with him.

'It's like you're my mum,' I'd say in frustration. 'And I'm like a child that needs to let go of your apron strings.' Tom hated me saying this and refused to believe it.

The trouble wasn't only that I needed to find myself, it was that I had gradually gained a hold over him in much the same way as I had over my mum all those years ago.

One afternoon Tom went out to visit one of his female friends. I expected him back after about an hour as she had M.E. and visitors were only allowed to stay for a short while because they exhausted her. After an hour or so had passed and he hadn't returned I started to get agitated. Two hours passed and I was furious, pacing about the house and smashing anything I could lay my hands on.

'Get a grip on yourself. What's the matter with you?' I thought to myself. I wasn't worried that he was being unfaithful to me as I trusted him implicitly, but rather I was overwhelmed with jealousy that he was spending time with anyone other than me.

He returned two hours later than I had expected. I waited in the kitchen, preparing the dinner, with a smile on my face, feeling calmer following my private outburst. 'Hi,' he said when he saw me. The sight of him brought back my fury and before I knew what I was doing I punched him hard in the stomach. I knew in that moment that there was something very wrong with me. I was deeply insecure and my fears often made me lash out indiscriminately.

But Tom continued to have faith that we could sort it out.

Tom tried to explain what splitting up would really mean. 'You realize this means that I'll be able to see other people,' he said. I didn't like that idea at all, but I put it to the back of my mind. I'd cope.

After two weeks, Tom had had enough of trying to talk me out of it. The more he went on, the more I closed off to him, and the easier it became for me to live with my decision. Nina will be fine, I thought.

Tom headed out to the pub to drown his sorrows and get away from the impossible situation. I was glad to be free from him. Nothing, absolutely nothing, could change my mind. Once it's made up, there's no going back.

I changed my mind.

Chapter Thirty-Seven

And Then It Was Gone

In early 2006 I became pregnant again. The home test was positive, so I made an appointment with the midwife, who worked out my due date and set me up with an appointment to have a scan. I was really pleased with the news, and Tom seemed enthusiastic about it, too.

After I decided to stay with Tom we worked hard at bonding again, spending more time together. As my relationship with Nina continued to improve I gained in confidence as a mother. This boosted me a great deal and in turn I relied less on Tom to support my fragile ego. It seemed right that we should have another child together. I had enjoyed being pregnant with Nina and looked forward to all the feelings that came with having a life grow inside.

By then, my job at the Post Office included a lot of heavy lifting, lugging the sacks I'd collected on my rounds into the depot. I thought it best to tell my boss the news immediately so that I'd be given light duties. He agreed, but I had to complete another week before they put me back in offices. From then on, I was in the sorting office, training to use the machinery and hand-sorting letters.

All seemed well until Tom, Nina and I went for a routine scan at the hospital. According to the calculations made by the midwife, it was twelve weeks since conception, so we were expecting the scanner to capture the unmistakable image of a tiny curled foetus. I lay on a couch in the window-less room, Tom by my side, as the doctor manoeuvred the machine into position. I unbuttoned my jeans and the cold gel was spread over my belly. The doctor began pressing the sensor across my lower abdomen, confidently explaining what we would see on the monitor. We knew, of course, having been through it with Nina.

He worked his way around, muttering to himself occasionally. It seemed to be taking a long time. He stopped, then tried the process again. Something was wrong. 'Are you sure you're pregnant?' he said at last.

Our nervous anticipation wasn't replaced with the excitement and joy we were expecting. Instead, there was just a crushing feeling of utter disappointment.

We were asked to wait in a room nearby until a nurse could talk to us. It seemed like a long time. When she arrived, she sat down and began explaining what we already knew only too well. I'd had a missed miscarriage. She handed us some pamphlets and dealt with the matter like a bereavement.

When she'd said her bit, we had another wait before seeing a doctor. He spelled out what my options were. What was left of the baby had to come out. I could have an operation that day, or wait to see if my body would perform the process naturally. It was too much to cope with at that moment and I said I'd like to go home and wait.

There was one thing he said that really troubled me. He said it was probable that the baby had stopped developing somewhere around the age of nine weeks. I had been lifting sacks at about that time, and I had the chilling realization that my exertions may have done the damage.

I went home, worried about what to expect. Would I be doubled up in pain with blood pouring out of me in the street? There was no way of knowing. It was just a case of waiting. A week later, nothing had changed and I went for another appointment. I was told that I could wait one week longer, but then it was recommended I have an operation.

Tom dropped me off at the hospital for the operation seven days later. I didn't want to imagine what was going to be done when I went under the anaesthetic, but it was impossible not to. I was taken into a room where I undressed and put on a gown. A nurse came in holding a cardboard tray with a single pill on it. I was told to insert it in me to soften the cervix ready for the vacuum. Soon after, the mask came down on my face and the next thing I knew, it was all over.

It took a couple of hours for me to recover enough to be allowed to go home. Tom had been waiting in the hospital for some time. He had Nina with him, so there was no chance for reflection. We just had to get on with our job as parents.

When we got home Nina threw up everywhere. It was one of the only times she'd ever been properly sick. I didn't want to ask Tom, so I just cleared it up myself and got on with making the dinner. I felt empty.

I took the miscarriage as an opportunity to re-evaluate my life. I was sick of working at the Post Office and wanted to spend more time with Nina. Because of the operation I had a sick note from the doctor, so I didn't have to work out my notice.

It seemed as though everyone there had known I was pregnant, so I couldn't face them now that I had lost the baby. I was paranoid that they might think I hadn't taken care of it. I went back only once, when I had to hand my uniform in.

I left there as I left everywhere I had worked: without saying goodbye.

My income from the Post Office had been reasonably good for a part-time job, so it was a bit of a blow for Tom to have to immediately try to fill the gap by finding new work. Only a week before, the magazine that provided him with most of his work had warned him that they were having to cut the page count significantly, so there would be fewer out-of-house commissions.

'If you want to leave the Post Office, that's OK,' he said. 'If I'm not looking after Nina in the afternoon, I can use that time to look for more work.'

There were tough times ahead.

Chapter Thirty-Eight

Playing by the Rules

After Nina was born, I was too busy being a mum to keep up my Steiner work, but I still harboured ideas of perhaps teaching in a Steiner school, and bringing Nina up by its principles. When I'd first got interested in Steiner, childcare became my obsession, which I fed with literature on the subject. I considered it to be superior to state schooling and got furious whenever I read about the national curriculum. But that was all theory. Nina was real, not a product to be shaped, and her existence started making me question what it was all about.

I began to realize that the Steiner philosophy on childcare was not the perfect guide to life I'd been looking for. It was a set of teachings with some very sound principles, but served out by flawed, obsessive people, like me. That's the problem with institutions that have a lot of rules; they seem to attract people who need rules in their lives to follow. I cringed when I remembered how I'd arrogantly dished out instructions to struggling mothers, when I actually had no children of my own.

For a time, I was friends with my Steiner assistant who was bringing up her children by applying all the Steiner principles by the book. It was like a mission for her. When Tom and I were visiting one day, over lunch she explained about her Catholic upbringing and how much she objected to the way it had repressed her. She wanted something different for her children, just as I was looking to the Steiner technique as a superior path to that of the Fellowship. She nearly had a coronary when she found Tom engaging her children in some competitive races in the garden, and acted as if his games would damage them irreparably. And yet, she would walk along holding her young son in one arm, puffing away on a rollup and sending clouds of smoke directly into his face.

I'd hoped Rupert, who I considered a friend, would be excited at the birth of my baby, but when I left he showed no interest in me, my life or, most importantly, Nina. He did come to the house occasionally, but not to have a cup of tea, see us, and find out how the baby was developing. There would be nothing more than a clatter of the letterbox, and a Steiner newsletter dropping on the mat. I'd see him cycle off down the road and that would be it.

Once I'd left the Steiner group, no one kept in touch. I was out and they were in. I thought I'd found the true path, I suppose. But I'd just replaced one institution following a set of rules with another.

Chapter Thirty-Nine

My Brother and Tom

I never lost contact with Victor, even when I was a teenager and he was a young adult living a worldly life, disapproved of by my parents. When I moved to Norwich he visited me at the clinic and wrote letters, and was never more than a phone call away.

Tom's first meeting with Victor was outside a coffee bar in Angel, Islington. Rupert had encouraged me to travel to London to attend a Steiner convention so that I could train to become a teacher, but the event turned out to be a disappointment. It seemed to be little more than a few tables in a small hall, selling educational books and providing information leaflets. The venue had proved to be difficult to find in the first place, and we soon left to have lunch, the plan being that Victor would join us in his lunch break. At that time he was the manager of a building firm nearby, and didn't have far to come.

I was excited about showing off my new boyfriend but also fearful of Victor's criticisms. He'd never been shy of coming forward with his opinion, and could be brutally blunt. My biggest fear was that the two wouldn't get on. I trusted Victor's opinions about people, and Tom's, too, so if they didn't like each other my loyalties would have been split.

I'm not sure how much they learned about each other that afternoon, but I think they were both relieved to have got the initial meeting under their belts. Still, both men were protective of me and viewed each other with a little suspicion.

They'd probably met only a handful of times before Tom bought his house, but, within the first year, Victor stayed for a week to look after things and have a break away from London, while we had a holiday. The lodger, Adam, kept himself to himself, hardly ever leaving his bedroom. In every way, Adam was the opposite of Victor, who found him hilarious. We left Victor a key so that he could let himself in after we'd gone. He'd been in the house for an hour or two before he heard a door open and Adam scurried down the stairs.

'I'm Lindsey's brother, you must be Adam,' said Victor.

'Oh, yeah, Lindsey said you were coming. I heard the door go earlier, but I didn't know if it was a burglar,' Adam mumbled.

'You didn't bother to find out, then?' Victor sniggered.

When I told him that I was pregnant with Nina, Victor didn't say much, which probably meant he was pleased. From that point on, he went out of his way to help us prepare the house in readiness. In the summer, Tom decided to reroof the house, which needed felt putting under the tiles to replace the underlying thatch of reeds that prevented the rain getting in. Like many of Tom's plans, it escalated, and he was soon ordering a Veluxe window so that the loft could be made into a room. Victor offered to help him do the work for free, and spent two weeks of his holiday staying with us while it was done.

It was a strange relationship up there on the roof. Victor got on with the task, cutting the lead work and edge tiles, while Tom helped him as a labourer's assistant would do. Yet Tom kept a close eye on progress, making sure no corners were cut. The more blasé Victor got, the more meticulous Tom became. Tom was just like his dad, Frank, in that respect, and (as Victor and I agreed) also quite like mine.

After Nina was born, Victor started visiting us in Norwich more often. He'd usually drive up from London just for the day, and then head to the coast for a walk on the beach. He didn't really speak much about what he got up to in his life, which I found frustrating. I wanted to know if he had a girlfriend, what he did at weekends and how he felt about the situation with Mum and Dad. But Victor was secretive and preferred to focus his attention on us and what we were doing. By this time he and Tom were getting on really well, particularly when they were discussing the latest DIY job Tom was planning.

If I needed any practical help, he was there for me, and would often send a little money as a present when the going got tough. Without a family of his own, ours became the closest thing he had.

Just before Nina was born, Victor came up to help with some more decorating work, and met Tom's dad, who was also lending a hand. The working atmosphere was a nicely informal way for Victor and Frank to meet, and they got along well. Tom's mum, Jane, really took to Victor, too, and it wasn't long before she invited him to join us all for Christmas. I wasn't sure how Victor would feel about it. Like me, he was affected by the Fellowship upbringing in so many ways, and it must have been a nerve-racking experience, entering a family's house during a celebration he hadn't grown up with. But Victor turned up, and it became a tradition for him to do so every Boxing Day.

If Victor hadn't been so much a part of my life, I'm sure I would have felt extremely isolated from my family. But, as my relationship with my parents became more restricted, in the summer of 2000 new family members unexpectedly entered my life. My cousin-in-law Danielle wrote to me to say that a message had been left on an ex-Fellowship member website, and it was addressed to Victor, Samantha, Alice and Lindsey. I had to find out what it said, but I had no idea about the Internet at that time. Tina had let me use her computer and helped me search for the message.

When we located the note, my heart was pumping with excitement. It was from Uncle Trevor and Uncle Roderick, and there was a telephone number for me to call. I couldn't believe that someone in the family was out there looking for me. I made the call, and, very soon after, I was exchanging emails with the two brothers.

They explained to me a little about the split in the Fellowship and how that had meant they'd not been able to speak to me, even though they wanted to. I suppose I gravitated towards Roderick because he was no longer in any part of the Fellowship. He was still devoutly religious, and even had a job working as the minister for a church, but that organization didn't impose restrictions on people's lifestyles in the same way.

Trevor, on the other hand, was still in the Open Fellowship, which wasn't something I wanted to have any involvement with, having worked so hard to distance myself from something similar.

The first meeting I had was with Roderick and his wife Brenda, who drove up from Kent to see me in my bedsit on

Magdalen Street. Their children, Chloe and Alec, didn't visit on that occasion, but my uncle showed me some photographs of them and spoke about his sister, my mum.

I scrutinized the couple who sat there in my room with suspicion. I wondered if they had some ulterior motive for making contact. I studied their dress closely, looking for evidences of Fellowship uniform, making sure they were normal in appearance. I was trying so hard to be worldly that I didn't feel I could afford to be seen with anyone who didn't blend in as well as I was trying to. I was prepared to be defiant, boldly puffing on a rollup and wearing my combat trousers. I wanted them to see my short hair, nose ring and stereo, and know that I was in no way receptive to any preaching.

I needn't have worried. Roderick and Brenda turned out to be two of the most accepting people I have ever met. I pushed my values in their face as much as possible, knowing that they were a challenge to their religious convictions, but they took it all in without passing judgement.

Our correspondence continued after that, and I made a trip to Kent to meet my cousins and Trevor's family, who were also surprisingly accommodating. Roderick and Brenda's visits to see me became regular, even though it was a long drive to make in a day. On one occasion they came to join me at a garden party, bringing Chloe and Alec with them. Most of the people there I knew from my group-therapy sessions, and so almost all had some major personal problem they were working through. It certainly wasn't what my family were used to, but they were willing to make whatever effort was necessary to understand and accept my life.

When I met Tom, they accepted my relationship with him, putting us up in their house, a vicarage, even though we weren't married. And, when Nina was two, we all went to stay at their new home for a few days. They would say a prayer at mealtimes, but we weren't made to take part.

One evening Tom questioned what Roderick believed, having seen the large glass-fronted book cabinet, stacked top to toe with theology texts. Tom explained his view on organized religion, which was pretty scathing, and his belief that there isn't a God. Roderick happily discussed it all.

I think Roderick felt an immense responsibility for me, as it was his sister who had put me in such a hopeless situation.

Chapter Forty

Testing Times

My miscarriage had shaken me up, and helped me wake up to how lucky I was to have a healthy daughter and a partner who loved me. I continued to struggle with my body issues and my sex life with Tom was intermittent. Nonetheless, we decided to try for another child. This was partly driven by Tom's concerns about Nina being an only child, like himself. He worried about her being lonely and said he'd hated not having any brothers or sisters to confide in when he fell out with his parents.

When I suspected that I was pregnant, I told Tom I wanted to test myself. He begged me to wait until he'd finished work so we could share the excitement together, but I went ahead. I'd had some sort of personal crisis the day before, involving my usual worries about my body and weight, and Tom had not been able to work while supporting me. Today, he was catching up, but I was feeling better, and immediately turned my thoughts to pregnancy. I walked to the nearest Boots the Chemist and bought a kit. I couldn't wait until I got home. In fact, I couldn't wait more than thirty seconds, and nipped into the grubby public toilets that were in the same shopping precinct. The room was illuminated by dim blue lights, which made it almost impossible to see the line on the appliance, but it was there.

'I did the test, I'm pregnant,' I told Tom as soon as I got in, hoping he'd immediately drop what he was doing and join me in my moment.

'That's great,' he said, but he seemed reserved, and I felt crushed. I tried to distract him, but he said he was worried about getting the work finished, as there was a deadline looming.

'We can talk about it later. Just let me get a bit more of this done. I can't relax until I do.'

I didn't really understand how he was feeling.

Chapter Forty-One

Sister and Brother

From the moment Nina learned to crawl, our two cats had been terrorized. Lady Cat usually made a sharp exit long before Nina got anywhere near, but Orwell preferred his sleep. This enabled Nina to close in on him and begin a series of experiments, pulling fur, screeching in his ears and prodding him to get a reaction.

'Get off him, Nina,' we shouted at least fifty times a day. Even Orwell's food wasn't safe from her. If it was within crawling distance, Nina would head straight towards it and start munching on the biscuits. Sometimes we'd see the cat shoot out of the house, looking extremely annoyed, only to find Nina behaving oddly. 'Odd' meant Nina was quiet. Then we'd notice some tiny prick marks on her forehead, behind the ear or on an arm. That was evidence of the cat having to defend himself from her excited advances.

Both cats instinctively knew she was a baby, though, and made allowances, putting up with treatment they would not tolerate from Tom or me. If Tom was using the flea comb, rounding the cats up to go to the vet or trying to feed a worm pill into their mouths, he'd usually end up looking as if he'd been dragged through a thorn bush.

Orwell was Nina's toy, as far as she was concerned, and she adored him completely. It looked as though he would never get a moment's peace from her for the rest of his life. That was until Stanley came along in 2007. She was all over her baby brother from the moment he was born, grabbing him and covering his soft, bald head with sloppy kisses.

Now all we seemed to be saying was, 'Get off his head, Nina!' from first thing in the morning to last thing at night. We'd expected jealousy. Nina had demanded our attention every moment of the day since she was born, and we'd been attending to her every whim like a couple of eager servants. Having Stanley around changed her role in the family overnight, but, instead of hating him, she put her arms around his shoulders, attached her lips to his head and pushed anyone away who came near.

Stanley was her baby brother – her plaything. Orwell was off the hook for the time being, and went back to the tiring business of sleeping.

We hadn't known what we'd do with Nina when I'd gone into labour. We weren't close enough to any of our neighbours to assume they'd be able to look after her for however long it took. My friend Lucy was on standby, but she had moved some twenty or more miles away to Cromer. She was great with Nina, so we knew we could rely on her if she was available.

Just as before, the due date came and went without so much as a twinge of pain. Why were our children so reluctant to be born? Just like his sister, Stanley sat around in my belly for a week longer than we expected. I was summoned for an appointment at the hospital so they could check me over, look at the health of the baby, and book me in for an inducement at the two-weeks-late mark, according to their rule on overdue babies. I really didn't want one of those, so I told the doctor that I'd had a sweep last time and that had done the trick.

On hearing this news, she performed a sweep, and within a couple of hours, not long after I got back home, I started going into labour. The first cramps began as I picked Nina up from playschool, but I didn't panic. I knew I had plenty of time. When I got back I told Tom that it was starting, but I still felt really calm, and had a sandwich for lunch.

There was nothing we could do for the next few hours. It was far too soon to call the midwives, and no way of knowing how long it would take before I was doubled up in pain. Nina wasn't quite three years old, so she had no idea what giving birth entailed. We carried on as normal for as long as possible.

Some time in the middle of the afternoon, I made the call to the midwives. By the time they arrived, I was in full-blown labour and Nina was wanting to know why I was yelling out in pain. Lucy had said she was on her way, but, until she got there, Tom had to sit with Nina in the back room. Everything was happening much faster than it had when Nina was being born, and Tom began to worry that the baby would pop out while he was out of the room.

'It's on its way, it won't be long now,' one of the midwives said to him. Lucy arrived at just the right time and took over, whisking Nina upstairs, reading her stories and getting her dressed for bed.

'Never again, I don't want to have another baby, Tom,' I whispered, as I squeezed his hand. As before, I'd adopted a kneeling position, but this time I was bent over a different chair a few feet away from the sofa. My new baby was going to be born in exactly the same spot as the last had been.

By eight o'clock in the evening, I was holding a baby boy. I looked down at him and knew I was in love. Something had changed in me.

Upstairs, Nina was still awake and we could hear Lucy trying her best to settle her.

'Shall I bring Nina down to see him?' said Tom excitedly.

'OK,' I agreed, and he rushed up to tell the girls the news.

It took us a few days to come up with a name. Just as we'd done with Nina, we decided to see what sort of child we had before picking something. Stanley just seemed to be the one that suited his personality.

I don't know if it was experience, but everything seemed so much easier with Stanley. Labour had been eight hours instead of eighteen, and as soon as he was born he started feeding without a fuss. Maybe it was just that he sensed how calm I was, and felt secure because of that. Nina had been constantly pushing the boundaries and fighting me. Stanley was laid back and accepting.

Mum and Dad managed to find an excuse to come up and see Stanley when he was just a few months old. They bought a wooden cot for him, and agreed with the Fellowship that it was fine to deliver this in person, along with some of my old toys.

After that, with no other reasons left to visit, Mum could only get on with the business of knitting beautiful jumpers and cardigans for the children, packing them up in bundles and posting them every six months or so. On seeing what Nina and Stanley were wearing, other parents would often squeal with delight, wishing they had parents like mine.

Chapter Forty-Two

Off the Peg

A few months after Stanley was born, my thoughts began to turn to my image problems. I was having a great time being a Mum without all the self-doubt I'd had the first time, and felt love for both my children, but I did not feel the same about myself.

When I looked in the mirror, I still saw a dowdy, bookish girl who resembled a powerful packhorse instead of a graceful gazelle. When Tom and I were watching television, we'd occasionally see actresses who we thought looked like me. It was clear that he saw me very differently from the way I saw myself.

I would always relate to the short, plain-looking girls, who find their man by being kind and working hard – the ones with a 'nice personality'!

'There's you!' Tom would say pointing to the screen.

'That one on the left?' I'd ask, referring to the plump girl with bad skin.

'No! The other one,' he'd laugh.

I thought he was being ridiculous. 'No way! She's really pretty. Do I really look like her? You're deluded.'

I always wanted to believe the worst, just to be on the safe side.

One morning, when Nina was at playschool and Stanley was sleeping, Tom sat me down to talk about my self-image. He had had an idea. He leafed through a catalogue of clothes, asking which ones I would love to wear. There were plenty of beautiful dresses, sexy skirts and glamorous tight tops, but those weren't the ones I picked.

'I'd love to be able to wear that, but I can't,' I kept saying. I thought I'd be a plain girl pretending to be a beautiful woman, someone to be mocked and laughed at.

'You can wear anything you like,' Tom insisted. 'If that's what you like, then you should buy it. You're not wearing clothes because you like them: you're wearing them because they're the ones you *think* you should wear.'

He said that, if I dressed and behaved in a sexy way, eventually it would start to feel right. I took some persuading, but the idea that I, Lindsey, could actually wear something sexy was tempting.

We went on a massive shopping spree over the next few weeks, heading around town, Tom holding Stanley while I tried on high-heeled, tight leather boots, little skirts and bright satin tops.

'Get what you really want, not what you think you should wear,' Tom kept saying, as I passed by all the things I liked and headed towards the sensible garments.

At home I dressed up in my new attire. It wasn't the Lindsey that I'd created, but the one I wished I could be. I didn't feel right, but, at the same time, it was what I wanted.

For a few months I kept it up. In the morning, I'd open the wardrobe, resist my urge to reach for something baggy and put on one of my new outfits instead. The hardest thing was dressing up when I knew I'd have to go to playschool and face all the other mums.

I ran through all the possible comments I thought they might make. It seemed to me that a mum should wear clothes to reflect her job as a mother and provider, not as a woman. I'd bought a pair of high-heeled olive-coloured shoes and forced myself to wear them, striding into the playground with Nina's pushchair. I wore bright summer skirts that dangerously billowed in the wind, and applied makeup every day.

The hard thing was remembering what I was trying to do, and towards the end of the year, in which I'd experienced the usual ups and downs, I was struggling. As Christmas approached, Tom and I received an invitation to a party, which we gladly accepted.

We hadn't been to anything like that for years, and I realized that I had nothing suitable to wear. I had never dressed up for a party. Unlike most of my friends, I hadn't spent hours chatting to Mum when I was a young girl about what pretty dress to wear to a disco or birthday party. The closest I had ever come to that kind of thing was asking Mum's opinion about whether I should wear the pink headscarf or the purple one when we went to a meeting.

As an early Christmas present, Tom said he'd buy me something for this occasion and others. I spent two hours in a shop, while Nina ran about and Tom played with Stanley. Of everything I looked at, Tom said, 'If you like it, try it.' There were only a few other customers, so we had staff members rushing back and forth, grabbing different sizes and cuts of dress. Tom was having a rare moment of carefree spending, and, by the time we'd finished, I had three new evening dresses, two formal ones that I could wear to interviews, plus several tops and yet another pair of shoes.

It seemed like too much, but Tom said that he'd had a couple of good months work wise, and it was to make up for many years of not buying much at all. I wore one of the dresses, a black one, and my new shoes to the party, which I really enjoyed. At one point I was cornered by someone who became fascinated with my upbringing. It always took me by surprise that other people found it so interesting. To me, it was just my life.

Chapter Forty-Three

Don't Turn Your Back on Me

We'd been muddling along as a couple for nine years, trapped in a situation where we had no money and two children to look after. I was prone to smashing things through clumsiness and rage, and Tom began to feel anxious that what little money was coming in was going on replacements. All it would take was a phone call to my mum, who I rang occasionally if only to tell her how the kids were doing, and something would get hurled at the wall.

'If you're not happy, Lindsey, then you've only got yourself to blame,' she'd say in a matter of fact way.

'It was your choice to leave the Fellowship. If only you'd let the Lord into your heart then He'll show you the True Path to real happiness.'

I became really enraged though when she said, 'You have to admit, Lindsey, the reason you got better from your anorexia is because the Fellowship prayed for you.' It infuriated me that she couldn't acknowledge that it was my hard work that had got me out of the clinic, into a position where I could have a loving family of my own. I didn't even bother to point out that I wasn't over my eating disorder, and every day was still a struggle.

I battered the ironing board with the iron, threw the phone across the room and destroyed an alarm clock. Tom would usually find a fragment of plastic or glass I hadn't swept up and twig what had happened.

I'd even take it out on Tom occasionally, but hitting him was like striking a brick wall and I usually just injured myself. He didn't seem to mind.

Tom's freelance work kept things ticking over, but every opportunity that presented itself turned to, as Tom would put it, 'rat shit'. It became a running joke between us that he was jinxed.

If he came downstairs enthusiastically talking about some possible work, I would have to hold back a grin.

'What?' he'd ask defensively.

'You know that whenever you get excited about something it all goes wrong.'

'I know, but I think this will be OK because ...' he'd quickly say, trying to convince himself as much as me.

Two weeks later the golden opportunity would indeed have turned to rat shit. But I was always too wrapped up in my own worries to imagine how he was feeling about that. I thought that, if things were going wrong for him, it was because there was something wrong with him. I didn't know what, but all I wanted to do was fit in with the world, and here I was with someone who was obviously not doing that. I struggled with my feelings of resentfulness.

The insecure part of me thought, why doesn't he just get a normal job and then we'd have some money? The caring side disagreed. It said, Tom is doing the work he enjoys, trying hard to make it a success. I respect his determination, and, in the end, that determination will pay off.

The problem was, it didn't take much to knock my confidence, and if that wobbled I lost all faith in what I really thought.

Tom hated the situation and was depressed. He felt tired all the time and rarely smiled. He also became short-tempered and so paranoid that if I made a joke he'd take it seriously and become defensive. I took it all to mean that he was off with me. We were slowly moving apart again but didn't realize.

My regular appointments with my therapist, Diane, were beginning to become more of a hindrance than a help. Rather than be brave and thrash out my worries and problems with Tom, I'd save them up to discuss in private with Diane. I realized that this wasn't helping, and it should be Tom I was telling some of these things to. Sometimes I'd go into a session feeling fine, without anything to say, but I'd come out obsessing about all the things we'd discussed; usually something to do with my upbringing in the Fellowship. We had got into a habit of going over ground that I had covered a thousand times, but because I was still extremely unhappy in myself and desperate to sort out my negative feelings, we kept thrashing it out.

It occurred to me that really I should stop looking backwards and concentrate on the good things in my life. I decided to stop going, and wrote a letter to Diane explaining my thoughts. I planned to speak to Tom about my worries from then on, but, instead, I just told no one at all.

It was in the autumn of 2008 and we took Nina and Stanley to Selattyn on the border between England and Wales. Tom and I had stayed in the same place before the children were born and really liked the area. It was nice to get away but, as with so many of our holidays, the weather was terrible. It rained almost every day and was freezing in the cottage. It felt like we were endlessly putting pound coins in the electricity meter, but we told ourselves that being on holiday was all about relaxing and tried not to worry about the money we were spending.

But, after we got back, work began to pick up for Tom, and it seemed as though the jinx was finally lifting. He was working most of the week for a distributor and getting even more magazine work than normal. The problem was, I was hardly seeing anything of him and was sick of the monotony of my life. I loved Stanley and Nina, but the routine was getting to me. Tom's mum and dad wouldn't take Stanley for any useful length of time because he was too young, so all I was doing was going to and fro, taking Nina to playschool.

I was convinced that Tom fancied other girls more than me, and I began to think he didn't want to be with me at all. He hardly came near me and always seemed to be complaining about something I'd done or not done. This made me feel tense so I picked at my skin and twitched. He complained about that, too. I couldn't seem to do anything right.

I didn't tell Tom of my dissatisfaction. I'm not sure I even admitted it to myself. But we were in a rut and only a great Christmas break could clear the air. At least we had money at last, and would be able to relax in that knowledge.

I know Tom was looking forward to a well-earned break, and I thought that a week at Tom's parents would help me put things in perspective. I got on well with both Frank and Jane and their calm attitude to life had a soothing effect on my own, often turbulent, existence.

Christmas was a disaster, not so much for me, but it felt that way to Tom, and his mood affected me. A couple of injuries had stopped him running the half-marathon he'd been planning; his three days' rest before Christmas were taken up fixing his computer; and then he came down with the flu the rest of us had just got over in time for the holiday. He spent the whole time in bed and then had to go back to work for the distributor straight afterwards. Come January, he was worse than ever.

It was then that I met someone. He was just a friend at first, someone I didn't find attractive, but had some annoying character traits which fascinated me. But he flattered me and that was it. I was soon addicted to the attention. Obsessed, for a while.

'I think it's over,' I said to Tom one evening in February. 'I just don't love you. I know I've said it before, but this time I'm sure. I'm just not excited by our relationship any more and I want to move out.'

I'd said it before, but this time I really meant it. I was seduced by my fantasies.

Tom was devastated and immediately started trying to find out what was wrong. I reeled off a long, long list of things I hated and resented him for. I'd been repressing how I felt for a long time and suddenly it was all pouring out. I wanted to hit him and hurt him. All at once it became clear to me that he was the source of all my problems. I shut myself off from him totally and felt nothing. It wasn't much to show for nine years.

At first Tom took all the blame. He was in shock and said he realized he'd not been treating me well. He said he did love me and wanted to be with me. I was suspicious. I didn't trust his motives. If he was being horrible to me, I didn't like it, and, if he was being nice, well, I didn't like that, either.

All I wanted was to get as far away as possible, and if it hadn't been for the children I would have packed up and left that very second. Not wanting Nina and Stanley to end up in some horrible rented accommodation, Tom offered to move out. He spent several nights staying with friends, while looking for somewhere to go.

Nothing was happening fast enough for me, though. I felt at last I had discovered the cause of my misery. I wanted instant closure, and the freedom to move on to the happiness that I was convinced was just waiting for me in the next chapter of my life. Victor had sold his business and wanted to invest some of his capital, so he agreed to help me buy a house for me and the children. I didn't want the children to lose their dad, so it had to be somewhere nearby. But nothing seemed to be going my way. Every property I liked was snapped up before I could put in an offer, or it was too expensive, and the ones that were available just weren't suitable for young children. Months had passed and I'd got nowhere. I was constantly stressed and smoking like a chimney.

Tom was still being nice. He said it was because he'd been shocked out of his depression and he had realized that his worries about money and work just didn't matter compared with what was going on. I didn't trust in what he was saying. He said he wanted me to stay, but was helping me move, and had even offered to go himself. Either way, I was beyond caring, I just wanted out. We'd been split but still living together for four or five months and there seemed no end to it.

'I wish you could take the children,' I said one day. 'Then I could just leave.'

It was a few days later that Tom said he'd been thinking about what I'd said.

'Maybe,' he began, 'I could look after the children.'

'How?' I gasped.

'Well,' he continued, 'if you can come over and look after them while I do my two days' regular work, I can drop some of the freelance stuff and take over childcare the rest of the time.' I talked through the details with him and he seemed to have it all worked out. Being the kind of person I am, I was looking for one-person flats within the hour, and had several viewings booked by the end of the day.

The first one I looked at was a depressing, soulless place I couldn't bear to consider. The second, however, was perfect. I took it straightaway and immediately began planning my new life. I'd already bought most of the things I needed. Every evening for months, when I wasn't out drinking with friends, looking for men, I'd sit at Tom's computer ordering kitchenware and furniture over the Internet. The bedroom had been stacked with boxes of the stuff for months.

Tom just seemed to put up with it all, but I didn't bother asking him how he felt. He'd let me have the bedroom and slept on a camp bed in a sleeping bag next to the children. He even helped me pack and move, taking apart my furniture at his end and assembling it at the other.

It broke my heart to leave the children behind, but it had been my decision to leave, not Tom's. I may have resented him, but I didn't really hate him. He didn't deserve to lose everything because of me. I knew he was a good dad and a better person for them to have around at that time. I was feeling like a sixteen-year-old, all over the place, not a responsible mum.

Tom still said he wanted me back, but said that he'd help me do what I wanted to do. I found this useful, and got him to plumb in my new washing machine and put up all my shelving and wall hangings. The problem was that I was addicted to using him to get things done. I'd ring up and kindly ask if he'd fix a light fitting, then get furious with him if he didn't dash over and do it straightaway.

'When are you coming to do this? You said you'd be over today,' I'd shout down the phone.

'I've got two children to look after, washing to do and food to cook,' he'd explain. 'I'll do it when I'm ready.'

He was starting to sound like a housewife.

The plan had been to stay friends, but I was finding it hard to do. I wanted to see other men and I knew it would upset him. I just didn't want to have to deal with that, and, because of the way we'd arranged our time, we were still seeing each other a lot and spending family days out. I wrote him a letter and left it for him at the house. I basically said that I wanted to stop our friendship and I'd devised a rota that meant we would meet only to hand over the children. Tom was upset, but I left him no choice.

Everything came to a head one day when I thought that I'd sussed out why Tom had been so nice. It came from just one thing that he said. He had just returned from his part-time work on the Monday, and was about to take over care of the children so I could head home to my flat for dinner.

'Thanks for looking after the children,' he said.

It seemed a strange thing to say. They are my children, I thought. Why are you thanking me for looking after them?

I began to suspect that he wanted to shut me out. Every so often I'd get the urge to rush over to see the children, so I'd call Tom up and say that I was on my way, but after I'd done this a few times he said it wasn't good for them or him.

'I'm trying to get a routine going, to create a stable life for me and the children,' he explained. 'I can't do that if you keep turning up whenever you feel like it. I need my own privacy too. I didn't want you to go, but now you have I just want to get on with things. You wanted us to have a rota, I'm just trying to stick to that.'

'You're trying to stop me seeing the children,' I suddenly found myself shouting. 'They're my children too. If you try I'll get a lawyer and we'll go to court.'

I'd really lost it, but, to be fair, a friend of mine who was being hounded by her ex-partner had made me suspect Tom's motives.

'You're a good man, Tom. I don't think you're trying to stop me seeing the children,' I said the next day.

Things calmed down after that. We still had the odd flare-up, though, usually because I felt compelled to keep saying, 'I don't love you, I don't want you, I don't fancy you,' every time I saw Tom, when 'Hello, how are you?' would probably have been better.

Occasionally this would rile Tom up to the point where he'd stamp around the house looking for something to hit that wouldn't cost the earth to fix. One time he dropped to the floor in frustration slamming his fists on the boards. Feeling that this was not relieving his pent-up emotion enough, he kicked one of the chairs across the room as hard as he could and stormed out of the house. He managed to get only halfway down the road before returning in agony saying, 'I think I've broken my foot.'

'Oh, Tom!' I said. It was difficult for us not to laugh at ourselves sometimes.

Before the move, I spoke to Mum on the phone and told her the news that we had split. She had one thing to say. 'It was bound to happen, Lindsey. You've continually refused to let the Lord Jesus into your heart.'

Our conversation was brief, but later on Dad called to give me a lecture, quoting huge sections of scripture. He obviously had it all planned out because, once he'd started, there was no stopping him. Tom was in the other room, but he could tell it was a call from my dad, just from hearing my exasperated comments. Tom came in to find out what was being said, so I silently mouthed, 'Listen to this!' He put his ear to the speaker and we laughed to ourselves. Dad might as well have been standing on that pitch outside Woolworth's.

I loved my flat. I'd got it just the way I wanted. Clean and tidy, a bit like my bedsit in the Close used to be, but with a more grown-up feel. It made me feel stressed when the children came round and turned it upside down. The plan had been for me to get set up so they could stay overnight, but I'd been slow in sorting out that part of the deal, so, whenever Tom wanted to go out, I had to babysit. I hated having to sit there waiting for him to roll in some time after midnight, but he was getting only one night off a week, and I could go out any time.

I certainly took advantage of my freedom a few times, but I still felt empty. It wasn't just because the children weren't there, although that was a large part of it. There was something else missing. The nights out began to lose their appeal. The world seemed full of people I didn't particularly want to meet, and that left me feeling hollow.

To make matters worse, Tom seemed to be losing interest. He'd finally got the message and was making new friends. He'd given up on chasing work and was just getting by looking after the children and socializing with other parents.

I began to wonder, What if I was wrong?

The summer holiday was drawing to a close and soon Nina would be starting her first year at school. I sat outside the house in the yard with Tom, who seemed distant but content. No longer was he trying to change my mind or pressurizing me. He was smiling again, and hadn't shown any irritation with my habits for six months or so.

Walking back to my flat that night I was surprised to realize that instead of feeling a wave of relief wash over me now that Tom had stopped saying he loved me, I felt strangely empty. 'If you don't love yourself, then you can't love anyone else.' The words that Tom had said to me so many times over the years crept back into my mind.

It suddenly struck me that I had exchanged loathing myself for loathing him. 'I haven't stopped hating myself,' I thought with horror. I just needed to believe I had. I couldn't live with being so unhappy with myself day in, day out and the protective shell that I had worked to build when I was little had become harder. I'd blocked out my negative feelings towards myself, and had once again turned against the one person who accepted and loved me for who I was: Tom.

Over the next few days, I didn't say anything to him about my changing feelings but let the idea run through my head that maybe, just maybe, I was wrong about him not being the right man for me. I thought about all times we had shared, the good and the bad. It occurred to me I wouldn't have wanted to have shared these moments with anyone other than Tom.

'Tom,' I said a couple of weeks later, as we puffed on our cigarettes in his back garden.

'Yes?' he replied.

'Would you consider having me back?'

There was a pause. I'd warned him nine and a half years ago that I was trouble and he should stay away. Now he'd finally got rid of me and had a chance of a happy life with someone less demanding and more stable.

'Erm, yeah,' he said.

'You bloody fool,' I said, grinning at him happily.

Chapter Forty-Four

Full Circle

We'll take it slowly, we agreed. I'd been at the flat for only three months, so there was half of my contract still to see out. Tom and I thought this was a good amount of time for us to get to know each other again before having to make a final decision. A lot of healing had to take place on both sides.

This time, we wouldn't rush into sex, and our physical separation would allow us the space we needed to build a healthy relationship before the intensity of living together. We were going to be sensible adults and get it right.

At least that was the idea. A tentative date or two, and we were having sex. It all seemed a bit fast, but I've never been any good at taking things slowly. 'More haste, less speed,' Tom was always saying to me, as I rushed around and he followed behind, picking up the pieces.

We asked Tom's mum and dad to take the children for a few days, saying that it was really important for us that they have Stanley as well, so we could sort some things out in our lives. They agreed.

I wasn't certain I was doing the right thing, but I had to give it another shot. Something had kept us together for nearly ten years. 'It must be worth fighting for,' I thought. Tom really had made changes, and I felt much more of an equal, having broken out on my own so definitively. I contacted my landlord, and let him know that I would not be renewing my contract after three months. He must have been relieved to get rid of me. I'd continually broken the terms of my contract by smoking inside and probably tortured the neighbours with my loud music.

On the day I told my landlord I didn't want to stay on there, he showed someone round. 'She wants to move in next week,' he said. 'Is that all right with you?' I took this as a sign that moving back with Tom was the right thing to do. If the process of moving out hadn't gone smoothly I'd have thought again.

A few days after that, my clothes and possessions were piled up in Tom's house. There was still a lot of furniture left at the flat, some of which I tried to sell to the new girl in an effort to claw back some of the three thousand pounds I'd spent moving out. Tom made good on his promise to let me have more space of my own and moved his studio into the attic, and we shifted the children's rooms around to make a better play area for them. I introduced a few new items of furniture from the flat and we both made an effort to get the place looking more homely than before.

We were making a new start, and so was Nina. Shortly after I returned, our little girl started school full time. I began a science module with the Open University and threw myself into the task with my usual single-mindedness. Tom carried on with his freelance work, regularly producing new and exciting leads that, inevitably, turned to rat shit, although this time it didn't worry him so much.

We had a great Christmas at Tom's parents' house, with Victor joining us on Boxing Day. And there was also a little competition I entered, which gave us something to get excited about …

As for my issues with food, well, they are still there, affecting every aspect of my life in some way or other. I have some terrible days when I can't see the point of carrying on, but I do, and I get through it. I still love my parents and sisters dearly and would like nothing better than to be able to have them as part of my life. But I have come to terms with the fact that I probably never will.

I have a family of my own and love Nina and Stanley more than I can say. As for Tom, well, I guess I love him too.

I don't believe in Heaven, God or the Devil any more. And, unlike my parents, I don't believe that this life has to be endured in order to get to a better place. For me, it's the here and now that is important. I know I have to get it right this time around. That is my goal, and maybe, some time in the future, I'll get there!

Afterword

'What was it like to grow up in a sect?' I have been asked this question many times over the years. What the question means is, 'What were the rules, what couldn't you do?' And so I tell them, but even to my ears it doesn't sound too bad. No TV, so what?

The damage that a sect like the Fellowship can do to a person is subtle, but long-lasting. Most people looking at my life as it is today will probably think that I have every reason to be happy, and I think so too. But as I wrote at the start of this book, 'The world, as we understand it, exists in our minds. The problem is, we all think differently.' The world I created in my head as a little girl, when I was forbidden from taking part in the real world beyond the Fellowship, is the one I still cling to for dear life. At first it was a place in which I lived out my fantasies, but that changed over time, and now it is one in which controlling my weight is the only thing that I believe stops it falling apart. That might sound mad, but that's what goes on. To look at me, you'd think I was perfectly well, but only Tom is witness to my struggles, and perhaps he is the only one who truly understands.

I know my children won't have to battle with the same kind of upbringing which damaged my life, and the life of my family, but I worry so much that the knock-on effects – my eating disorder – could be even more destructive. And so, I have prepared a letter for my daughter.

July 2010

Dearest Nina,

From the moment you were born my determination to recover from my eating disorders strengthened.

'I mustn't pass on my body issues to you,' was all I kept thinking.

Over the first year of your life you showed me what it is to be human. I felt angry at you a lot of the time because I found it hard to look after you and play when my head was filled with negative thoughts about myself. Sometimes I'd even shout at you in my frustration, but you continued to love me in spite of this. 'Don't worry mum,' you'd say when you were old enough to understand my frequent apologies for my horrible behaviour, 'I'll always love you.'

Every day you show me how it is possible to live without anxieties the way we look, 'I'll wear this mum,' you'll say, holding up a mismatching selection of clothing, and I hide my smile, delighted that you feel confident in your own style.

When I feel like giving up the fight to be free of the destructive rules that I live my life by, your smiles and care-free laughter inspire me to carry on.

Not a day passes when I don't silently thank you for being you.

I love you so much,
Mummy x

Acknowledgements

I would like to thank my parents, who, despite our differences, have shown me that it is important to stand by your beliefs.

Thanks also to my Uncle and Aunt who have accepted me without judgement; this means more than I can say.

Thanks to Tom for letting me use the lyric 'Tailor me, dummy' (from his song 'Off the Shelf'), and also his much appreciated and valued support during the writing of this book.

I would like to thank the BBC and HarperTrue for giving me the opportunity to tell my story.